FREEDOM OF EXPRESSION

OTHER TITLES IN THE
UNDERSTANDING CANADIAN LAW SERIES

YOUTH AND THE LAW

FREEDOM
OF
EXPRESSION

UNDERSTANDING CANADIAN LAW

DANIEL J. BAUM

DUNDURN
TORONTO

Editor: Michael Melgaard
Design: Laura Boyle
Cover Design: Carmen Giraudy
Printer: Webcom

Library and Archives Canada Cataloguing in Publication

Baum, Daniel Jay, 1934-, author
    Freedom of expression / Daniel J. Baum.

(Understanding Canadian law)
Includes bibliographical references and index.
Issued in print and electronic formats.
ISBN 978-1-4597-2317-7 (pbk.).--ISBN 978-1-4597-2318-4 (pdf).-- ISBN 978-1-4597-2319-1 (epub)

1. Freedom of expression--Canada. 2. Canada. Canadian Charter of Rights and Freedoms. 3. Canada. Supreme Court.

I. Title. II. Series: Understanding Canadian law (Toronto, Ont.)

KE4418.B38 2014   342.7108'53   C2014-902130-5
KF4483.C524B38 2014   C2014-902131-3

1   2   3   4   5   18   17   16   15   14

 Conseil des Arts   Canada Council
du Canada   for the Arts

ONTARIO ARTS COUNCIL
CONSEIL DES ARTS DE L'ONTARIO
an Ontario government agency
un organisme du gouvernement de l'Ontario

We acknowledge the support of the **Canada Council for the Arts** and the **Ontario Arts Council** for our publishing program. We also acknowledge the financial support of the **Government of Canada** through the **Canada Book Fund** and **Livres Canada Books**, and the **Government of Ontario** through the Ontario Book Publishing Tax Credit and the **Ontario Media Development Corporation**.

Care has been taken to trace the ownership of copyright material used in this book. The author and the publisher welcome any information enabling them to rectify any references or credits in subsequent editions.
J. Kirk Howard, President

The publisher is not responsible for websites or their content unless they are owned by the publisher.

Printed and bound in Canada.

Visit us at

Dundurn.com | *@dundurnpress* | *Facebook.com/dundurnpress* | *Pinterest.com/dundurnpress*

Dundurn
3 Church Street, Suite 500
Toronto, Ontario, Canada
M5E 1M2

Gazelle Book Services Limited
White Cross Mills
High Town, Lancaster, England
L41 4XS

Dundurn
2250 Military Road
Tonawanda, NY
U.S.A. 14150

For Penelope

CONTENTS

ACKNOWLEDGEMENTS

First, I would like to acknowledge the Supreme Court of Canada. Over the decades, the membership of this nine-person Court has altered through retirement (mandatory at age seventy-five) or death. Increasingly, the Court has tried to hand down judgments that come ever closer to being decisions that can be read, understood, and discussed by those who want to be informed about the structure of our law, of our government, and more importantly, of our society's values. So, I thank — most profusely — the Supreme Court of Canada.

A second link in the chain between the law and the people is the media. It is possible, of course, in our highly computerized society to read the decisions of the Supreme Court of Canada online, but that can be an arduous process. On occasion, magazines such as *Maclean's* feature a particular subject for investigative reporting in which the Supreme Court of Canada's judgments (such as those relating to tobacco) may form a part. Newspapers such as the *Toronto Star* may select a story reflecting a matter of social concern, such as bullying. And, on a daily basis, radio or television may report on such stories.

The net effect of media reporting, at best, ranges from episodic to minimal. Perhaps the one constant to which we frequently refer in this series is the informed editorials in Canada's national newspaper, the *Globe and Mail*. Without hesitating, the *Globe and Mail* granted the right to reprint editorials (and there were many) on Supreme Court of Canada decisions. The approach of the *Globe and Mail* seems to be: Let the public be made aware. I thank them for their generosity and for maintaining consistently high standards.

Ordinarily, I would say that I take full responsibility for the contents of this book. Hopefully, however, the contents do not reflect my judgments but those of the Supreme Court of Canada. My task, as I saw it, was to discuss those judgments in a non-judgmental and accessible way.

INTRODUCTION

There are limits to what we can say and how we can express ourselves. It may be no more than a prank, but the law likely will come down with a heavy hand on the person who simply wants to see what will happen if she shouts "Fire!" in a crowded theatre. For her it may be no more than speaking freely, "letting herself go." For the public — frightened or injured rushing from the theatre in response to the shout — the act is careless. The state might hold the shouter criminally responsible. And those injured might even seek damages against her.

Between the right to speak or express oneself and demonstrable harm that such speech or action may cause, there is a wide area in which courts, and especially the Supreme Court of Canada, set boundary markers that, on the surface, seem clear and simple. They are embedded in the highest law of the land, the Charter of Rights and Freedoms, part of the Constitution of Canada. Section 2 of the Charter states:

2. Everyone has the following fundamental freedoms:
   (a) freedom of conscience and religion;
   (b) freedom of thought, belief, opinion and expression, including freedom of the press and other media of communication;

(c) freedom of peaceful assembly; and

(d) freedom of association.

The difficulties are not in the principles, but in their application. The principles must be applied to individual situations, to facts that often reflect "legitimate" values other than those of freedom of expression. How are these values to be weighed? How are courts to decide? The facts become enormously important.

School classrooms are supposed to be places of learning. Does this allow school authorities to express points of view that may be seen as discriminatory toward a particular group? For example, if religious belief requires Sikh males to wear a kirpan (a dagger) as an expression of their faith, may school boards prohibit such action in the interest of school safety?

Freedom of expression principles can come into play in numerous settings. In this book, we show the stretch of the law in balancing the fundamental right of freedom of expression against other legitimate interests of government, especially as seen by the Supreme Court of Canada.

WHO ARE THE JUDGES?

A few words must be said about the judges (or justices, as Supreme Court of Canada judges are called). Who are they? How are they chosen? How do they go about coming to decisions? The answer to these questions may help us better understand the decisions that we will be examining.

In 1989 Beverley McLachlin, then chief justice of British Columbia, received a telephone call from the prime minister of Canada. He asked if she would consider a new position: that of a justice of the Supreme Court of Canada.

It was within the power of the prime minister, accepted by his Cabinet, to offer the position. The appointment of a justice of the Supreme Court of Canada did not have to go through parliamentary committee or parliamentary consent, as such — a process enormously different from that of the United States, where the president nominates and the Senate, following hearing, either gives the nomination a stamp of approval or rejection. (If the Senate rejects, then the candidacy of that person comes to an end.)

Justice McLachlin thanked the prime minister, accepted his offer, and became a justice of the Supreme Court of Canada. On January 7, 2000, the prime minister offered Justice McLachlin the position of chief justice of the Supreme Court, and she accepted.

There are nine justices who make up the Supreme Court of Canada. The conditions for their appointment are few, but they are important. They are appointed through the prime minister and the Governor in Council. In this regard, the "pool" for appointment by law is comprised of superior court judges or barristers with at least ten years in practice in a province or territory.

Once named to the Supreme Court, a justice cannot be removed from office so long as the justice carries out her/his duties in accordance with the law. But, at the age of seventy-five, there is forced retirement. (However, many retired justices are called back to serve in appointments such as chairing special commissions.) A serving justice can only be removed from office for bad conduct or incapacity (such as illness).

By law, the prime minister is required to appoint three justices from Quebec. By tradition, the prime minister also appoints three justices from Ontario, two from the West, and one from Atlantic Canada.

How the prime minister goes about selecting a justice for the Supreme Court, given the broad limits described, is for the prime minister to determine. In 2012 Prime Minister Stephen Harper set new guidelines. He named a panel of five members of the House of Commons: three Conservatives (the prime minister's governing party), one New Democrat, and one Liberal. Their task was to review a list of qualified candidates put forward by the federal justice minister in consultation with the prime minister, the chief justice of the Supreme Court of Canada, the chief justice of Quebec (where the next justice was to be selected), the Attorney General of Quebec, and provincial and territorial bar associations (as well as public suggestions).

The panel was instructed to submit a list of three recommended candidates — unranked — to the prime minister and he would select one from that list. A public hearing before a special parliamentary committee would be held before the prime minister finalized the appointment.

The first justice selected through the process described above was Richard Wagner, who was a long-time trial lawyer before becoming a justice of the Quebec Court of Appeal. In an interview with the *Globe and Mail*, Justice Wagner said: "I might surprise you, but I liked the [hearing] process. There is nothing to hide. I think a judge should follow the directions of society, and that means to explain to citizens what we do, how we do it and why we do it. I think it's fair and it's reasonable."

A central concern, said Justice Wagner, is ensuring access to the justice system for all Canadians.

SOME FACTS

On the whole, it can be said that justices of the Supreme Court of Canada historically do not like to talk about themselves. But, there are some facts that may give rise to questions going to the makeup of the Court:

- There have been no persons "of colour" appointed to the Supreme Court of Canada.
- There have been no persons from among the "first peoples" (First Nations, Métis, and Inuit) appointed to the Supreme Court of Canada.

The fact is that white men, drawn from an elite part of the legal profession, constituted the "pool" from which justices of the Supreme Court of Canada were drawn — at least until 1982. In that year — at the time the Charter of Rights and Freedoms, an important part of the Constitution of Canada, came into effect — the prime minister named the first woman to the Supreme Court: Bertha Wilson. She had immigrated to Canada with her husband John, a Presbyterian minister in Scotland, in 1949.

Justice Wilson had received an M.A. in philosophy at the University of Aberdeen. Once in Canada, she applied for admission to the law program at Dalhousie University in Halifax. She recalled an interview with the dean of the law school, and chuckled about it later. The dean advised her to "go home and take up crocheting." She didn't. She entered the Dalhousie law program in 1955 and was called to the Nova Scotia Bar after graduation.

In 1959 Justice Wilson moved to Toronto where she found employment with a leading law firm and later became head of research for that firm. Her job consisted in no small measure in writing opinions for members of the firm — a task that went a long way toward preparing her for work as a judge.

Justice Wilson received an invitation in 1979 to sit as a judge on the Ontario Court of Appeal. Her immediate response was surprise — and then laughter when, as a judge whose opinions reflected women's rights, she said: "I'll have to talk it over with my husband." She accepted the position on the Court of Appeal and served there until her appointment to the Supreme Court of Canada.

Justice Wilson was a Supreme Court justice from 1982 to 1991, retiring at the age of sixty-eight. There, she had an important role in interpreting the then newly-established Charter of Rights and Freedoms, including decisions relating to a woman's right to abortion (*The Queen v. Morgentaler* [1988] 1 *Supreme Court of Canada Reports* 30) and a spouse's right to claim self-defence to murder based on physical abuse by her/his spouse (called in law the battered wife syndrome) (*The Queen v. Lavallée* [1990] 1 *Supreme Court of Canada Reports* 852).

Since the appointment of Justice Wilson, a number of women have served as justices of the Supreme Court of Canada. In 2012, after serving as a justice for what she called ten "intense" years, Justice Marie Deschamps of Quebec resigned at the age of fifty-nine. (At that time, there were four women sitting as justices.) In an interview with CBC News a week after her resignation, Justice Deschamps was asked about "gender balance" on the Court. She answered, "I think every court should aim for half and half.... It's important that [the Court] is balanced.... I hope that the government will maintain at least four women on the Court.

Whether the next candidate is a woman or it's the one that follows it will be for the government to decide."

In fact, the prime minister named Justice Richard Wagner of Quebec to the Court, thus lowering the number of women justices (at least for the time) to three.

It should be noted that the chief justice at the time of Justice Deschamps's resignation was Beverley McLachlin (*CBC.ca*, August 15, 2012).

HOW ARE JUDGES TO DECIDE?

May emotion play a role in decision-making? For us, in reviewing decisions of the Supreme Court of Canada (or the decisions of any court, for that matter), an important question is whether justices can decide a case largely on the facts and the law as given. Can they remove (or largely isolate) any individual bias?

There are two parts to the answer — at least as applied to the Supreme Court of Canada:

1. No single justice decides a case. If the Court sits as a panel, there usually are seven justices who meet, discuss, and work toward an opinion which the chief justice usually assigns to a specific justice. If there is disagreement that cannot be otherwise resolved, then the way is open to a written dissent or a concurring opinion. (Often the justices are able to work out their disagreement to form a majority or a unanimous opinion.)
2. A case may be one that summons enormous emotion. Such was the case of Robert Latimer, a Saskatchewan farmer charged and convicted in the "mercy" killing of his disabled daughter. Twice the case went on appeal to the Supreme Court of Canada. The second time, the appeal was from a judgment of the Saskatchewan Court of Appeal that had increased a sentence of one year to ten years.

In a decision by the Court as a whole in the Latimer case — not one attributed to any particular justice — the Supreme Court of Canada affirmed the judgment. The role of emotion in coming to decision was lessened.

Justice Ian Binnie, on his retirement after serving fourteen years on the Court, commented on the Latimer case in an extensive interview with Kirk Makin of the *Globe and Mail*:

> The Robert Latimer case was a hugely controversial case, but to me, the legal outcome was straightforward. You can't have people making their own judgments as to whether their child should live or die.
>
> In saying that, I make no moral judgment about what Latimer did. I accept his word that he did it because he thought it was best for his daughter.
>
> But the legal decision wasn't his to make. But the law is clear. When you talk about judges applying the law and not making it up, if the Criminal Code is clear about the penalty that follows from the crime of homicide, then that is the penalty that follows. You can't apply the law differently from case to case depending on a judge's personal view of whether a constitutional exemption is warranted.
>
> So, there is no necessary [relation] between how much you agonize over a decision and what the moral implications or the controversy is outside the courtroom. My only function in that case is the right legal result. In that case the legal result was clear. My personal views of whether it was a good outcome or a bad outcome were irrelevant (*Globe and Mail*, September 23, 2011).

REFERENCES AND FURTHER READING

Fitzpatrick, Meagan. "Supreme Court Should Have Four Women Says Retiring Justice," *CBC.ca*, August 15, 2012.

Makin, Kirk. "Justice Ian Binnie's Exit Interview." *Globe and Mail*, September 23, 2011.

_____. "Supreme Court Judge Warns of 'Dangerous' Flaws in the System." *Globe and Mail*, December 12, 2012.

CHAPTER 1

ADVERTISING: FROM POLITICAL ACTIVISTS TO GRAFFITI ARTISTS

The major case discussed in this chapter illustrates the principle of freedom of expression and the difficulties of "detail" in applying that principle. The case was a unanimous judgment from the then eight-member Supreme Court of Canada (*Greater Vancouver Transportation Authority and Canadian Federation of Students — British Columbia Component, and British Columbia Teachers Federation, and the Attorney General of British Columbia,* 2009 *Supreme Court of Canada Reports* 31). We shall call it the bus case.

Students and teachers wanted the right to buy advertising panel space on buses operated by the authorities that were controlled by the city government. As a matter of "policy," their request was denied. The students and the teachers went to court. They wanted a declaration that the denial was a violation of their Charter right to freedom of expression.

Among the questions raised in this chapter are:

- Does the city have a right to control how its buses will be used?
- Do the rights set out in section 2(b) of the Charter impose duties only on government?

- On what terms, if any, must the city sell advertising space to the students and the teachers?
- Can the city set standards that advertisers must meet?
- If the advertising attacks others, should there be a legal right to reply?

THE FACTS OF THE BUS CASE

The Greater Vancouver Transportation Authority (TransLink) and British Columbia Transit (BC Transit) are corporations that operate public transportation systems in British Columbia. TransLink is responsible for running the transit system in the area under the authority of the Greater Vancouver Regional District (GVRD). BC Transit operates in British Columbia communities outside the GVRD. For years, the "transit authorities" have earned revenue by posting advertisements on their buses.

In the summer and fall of 2004, the Canadian Federation of Students — British Columbia Component (CFS) and the British Columbia Teachers' Federation (BCTF) — tried to buy advertising space on the sides of transit authority buses. The CFS, a society that represents thousands of college and university students in B.C., wanted to encourage more young people to vote in a provincial election scheduled for May 17, 2005, by posting, on buses, ads about the election. The first ad, which was to run the length of the bus, would have depicted a silhouette of a crowd at a concert with this text:

Register now. Learn the issues. Vote May 17, 2005.
ROCK THE VOTE BC.com

The second ad was a "banner ad" to be placed along the top of the bus that would have had one long line:

Tuition fees ROCK THE VOTE BC.com
Minimum wage ROCK THE VOTE BC.com
Environment ROCK THE VOTE BC.com

The BCTF, a society and trade union that represents more than forty thousand public school teachers in B.C., sought to voice its concern about changes in the public education system. Its ad would have stated:

> 2,500 fewer teachers, 114 schools closed.
> Your kids. Our students. Worth speaking out for.

Both transit authorities refused to post the ads because they were contrary to their advertising policies. The transit authorities had adopted essentially identical advertising policies, which stated:

> 2. Advertisements, to be accepted, shall be limited to those which communicate information concerning goods, services, public service announcements and public events.
>
> ...
>
> 7. No advertisement will be accepted which is likely, in the light of prevailing community standards, to cause offence to any person or group of persons or create controversy.
>
> ...
>
> 9. No advertisement will be accepted which advocates or opposes any ideology or political philosophy, point of view, policy or action, or which conveys information about a political meeting, gathering or event, a political party or the candidacy of any person for a political position or public office.

The Supreme Court of Canada gave its decision five years after the attempts were made to place the ads on the buses. Many of the events giving rise to the requests for the ads had passed. Still, the case went forward. The students and the teachers wanted a court declaration that they had a Charter right to buy advertising on Vancouver-owned buses.

THE SUPREME COURT RULING

The Court unanimously agreed that the Vancouver transportation policy forbidding political advertising, as stated above, was a violation of section 2(b) of the Charter's right to freedom of expression. In this regard, the Court, through its opinion given by Justice Deschamps, stated that the violation could not be overridden by section 1 of the Charter. That is, the city government had not demonstrated that the limitation in its advertising policy was a reasonable limit that could be demonstrably justified in a free and democratic society. Thus, the limits set out in the transportation policy were not valid.

At the start, the Court stated that neither the teachers nor the students were barred from buying bus advertising. The prohibition came in terms of what they wanted to say in that advertising. Here the Court drew a distinction between government support of the activity of the teachers and students, and government simply making its bus panel advertising space available as it had done for others for several decades.

SECTION 2(B) OF THE CHARTER

Justice Deschamps, speaking for the Supreme Court of Canada, stated: "The [teachers and students] seek the freedom to express themselves — by means of an existing platform they are entitled to us — without undue state interference with the content of their expression. They are not requesting that the government support or enable their expressive activity by providing them with a particular means of expression from which they are excluded."

Justice Deschamps went on to spell out the application of section 2(b) of the Charter to the proposed bus advertising:

> The very fact that the general public has access to the advertising space on buses is an indication that members of the public would expect constitutional protection of their expression in that government-owned space.
>
> Moreover, an important aspect of a bus is that it is by nature a public, not a private, space. Unlike the activities which occur in certain government buildings or offices, those which occur on a public bus do not require privacy and limited access. The bus is operated on city streets and forms an integral part of the public transportation system.
>
> The general public using the streets, including people who could become bus passengers, are therefore exposed to a message placed on the side of a bus in the same way as to a message on a utility pole or in any public space in the city. Like a city street, a city bus is a public place where individuals can openly interact with each other and their surroundings. Thus, rather than undermining the purposes of section 2(b), expression on the sides of buses could enhance them by furthering democratic discourse, and perhaps even truth finding and self-fulfillment.
>
> In sum, this is not a case in which the Court must decide whether to protect access to a space where the government entity has never before recognized a right to such access. Rather, the question is whether the side of a bus, as a public place where expressive activity is already occurring, is a

location where constitutional protection for free expression would be expected.

I do not see any aspect of the location [bus panel advertising] that suggests that expression within it would undermine the values underlying free expression. On the contrary, the space allows for expression by a broad range of speakers to a large public audience and expression there could actually further the values underlying section 2(b) of the Charter. I therefore conclude that the side of a bus is a location where expressive activity is protected by section 2(b) of the Charter.

SECTION 1 OF THE CHARTER

The city government claimed that its advertising policy was adopted to "provide a safe, welcoming public transit system." This objective, the city government stated, warranted placing limits on freedom of expression.

Justice Deschamps accepted the validity of the transit policy. The difficulty the Court saw was a rational connection between that policy and denying the students and teachers the right to purchase advertising space for the messages set out or, more generally, for *political advertising*. Justice Deschamps stated:

I accept that the [advertising] policies were adopted for the purpose of providing "a safe, welcoming public transit system" and that this is a sufficiently important objective to warrant placing a limit on freedom of expression. However, ... I am not convinced that the limits on political content imposed by articles 2, 7 and 9 [of the transit authorities' policies] are rationally connected to the objective. I have some difficulty seeing how an advertisement on the side of a bus that constitutes political speech might create a safety risk or an unwelcoming environment for transit users.

It is not the political nature of an advertisement that creates a dangerous or hostile environment. Rather, it is only if the advertisement is offensive in that, for example, its content is discriminatory or it advocates violence or terrorism — regardless of whether it is commercial or political in nature — that the objective of providing a safe and welcoming transit system will be undermined.

Had I found a rational connection between the objective and the limits imposed by articles 2, 7 and 9, I would nevertheless have concluded that the means chosen to implement the objective was neither reasonable nor proportionate to the respondents' interest in disseminating their messages pursuant to their right under section 2(b) of the Charter to freedom of expression.

The policies allow for commercial speech but prohibit all political advertising. In particular, article 2 of the policies limits the types of advertisements that will be accepted to "those which communicate information concerning goods, services, public service announcements and public events," thereby excluding advertisements which communicate political messages.

Article 7, on the other hand, refers to prevailing community standards as a measuring stick for whether an advertisement is likely "to cause offence to any person or group of persons or create controversy." While a community standard of tolerance may constitute a reasonable limit on offensive advertisements, excluding advertisements which "create controversy" is unnecessarily broad. Citizens, including bus riders, are expected to put up with some controversy in a free and democratic society. Finally, article 9 represents the most overt restriction on political advertisements, as it bans all forms of political content regardless of whether the message actually contributes to an unsafe or unwelcoming transit environment. In sum, the policies amount to a blanket exclusion of a highly valued form of expression in a public location that serves as an important place for public discourse. They therefore do not constitute a minimal impairment of freedom of expression.

LIMITING BUS ADVERTISING

Question: Does the ruling in the bus case mean that government cannot limit bus advertising?
Answer: No.

Justice Deschamps, speaking for the Court, was clear on this point. Drawing an analogy to tobacco advertising and criminal law sanctions against indecency, she wrote:

> A limit that is not justified in one place may be justified in another. And the likelihood of children being present matters, as does the audience's ability to choose whether to be in the place. In *Canada (Attorney General) v. JTI-Macdonald Corp.*, [2007] 2 *Supreme Court of Canada Reports* 610, at paras. 93–94, one of the provisions at issue limited tobacco advertising that was appealing to young people or was published in places frequented or publications read by young people. This provision

was held to be justified on the basis of the need to protect youths because of their vulnerability.

In the criminal law context, this Court has held that the concept of indecency in the Criminal Code depends in part on location in that conduct that is indecent in one place may not be indecent in another more private place: [*The Queen*] v. *Labaye*, [2005] 3 *Supreme Court of Canada Reports* 728, at paras. 42–43; [*The Queen*] v. *Tremblay*, [1993] 2 *Supreme Court of Canada Reports* 932, at pp. 960–61.

In effect, Justice Deschamps said, advertising on buses has become a widespread and effective means for conveying messages to the general public. In exercising their control over such advertising, the transit authorities failed to minimize the impairment of political speech, which is at the core of section 2(b) protection. The Supreme Court concluded that, to the extent that articles 2, 7, and 9 prohibit political advertising on the sides of buses, they place an unjustifiable limit on the [students' and the teachers'] right under section 2(b) of the Charter to freedom of expression.

ANOTHER POINT OF VIEW

An editorial published in the *Globe and Mail* on July 11, 2009, took a position different from that of the Supreme Court of Canada in the bus case:

A city bus is not a democracy wall. The Supreme Court of Canada seems to think it is. It has just said — unanimously — that the Canadian Charter of Rights and Freedoms requires that public bus companies allow their advertising space to be used for political advocacy.

So here is a young woman, on her way to have an abortion. Her bus pulls up. From front to back is an advertisement from an anti-abortion group, likening what she is about to do to an act of murder. Does she feel comfortable on that bus?

Or there is a war in the Middle East. "Stop Israel's Gestapo Tactics," reads the ad. The next bus pulls up. "Stop Arab Terrorism," it says. Do the passengers feel comfortable on that bus?

Of course they don't. And it's not as if they can simply turn the page in a newspaper if an advertisement offends them. Many of them are "captive" passengers who can't afford cars or taxis. They're on the bus because they don't have a choice.

The bus companies involved in the Supreme Court case — the Greater Vancouver Transportation Authority and British Columbia Transit — are in a better position than the Supreme Court to understand the sensibilities of their customers. Their policy allows for commercial ads, not political ones, to preserve "a safe, welcoming public transit system." The Supreme Court conceded that the goal is praiseworthy, but "it is difficult to see how an advertisement on the side of a bus that constitutes political speech might create a safety risk or an unwelcoming environment for transit users."

One pictures the judges sitting around their oak conference table scratching their heads over the nature of a bus, somewhat in the manner of the blind-men-and-the-elephant parable.

Public transit companies need revenue, and so they advertise; the usual commercial considerations around their customers' sensibilities should apply. Instead the Supreme Court has denied them the discretion "not to publish" as they see fit, a discretion common among the privately owned media. The result, as Madam Justice Mary Southin of the B.C. Court of Appeal said three years ago in dissent [in the bus case], "is to diminish the dignity of the Charter, the underlying purpose of which, surely, was to protect the citizen from oppression by those set in authority over him." A bus is no longer just a bus, and the Charter is not quite the same Charter, either (*Globe and Mail*, July 11, 2009).

A MATTER OF APPLICATION

Question: Does the Charter impose duties on private businesses? **Answer:** No. The Charter applies to government. Section 32 of the Charter states: "This Charter applies (a) to the Parliament and government of Canada in respect of all matters within the authority of Parliament including all matters relating to the Yukon Territory and Northwest Territories; and (b) to the legislature and government of each province in respect of all matters within the authority of the legislature of each province."

Suppose in the bus case that the provincial government, in effect, privatized bus transportation in the greater Vancouver area. Assume that this was done by establishing two separate and completely independent corporations where the full ownership was held by residents of British Columbia through their government. The corporations, under our facts, were subject to the same laws as any other corporation or business in the province.

Now assume that the new corporations established the same rule as the previously operated bus authorities: No advertising space would be sold where the object is political solicitation.

Would the new corporations be subject to the Charter?

A CHARTER-FREE ZONE?

In the bus case, the Supreme Court of Canada gave section 32 a broad interpretation to embrace Charter protection. The Court stated: "On the face of the provision, the Charter applies not only to Parliament, the legislatures and the government themselves, but also to all matters within the authority of those entities."

The Court then cited its earlier decision in *Godbout v. Longueuil (City)*, [1997] 3 *Supreme Court of Canada Reports*, 844, where Justice Gérard La Forest explained the reasoning for the broad reach of section 32:

> Were the Charter to apply only to those bodies that are institutionally part of government but not to those that are — as a simple matter of fact — governmental in nature (or performing a governmental act), the federal government and the provinces could easily shirk their Charter obligations by conferring certain of their powers on other entities and having those entities carry out what are, in reality, governmental activities or policies. In other words, Parliament, the provincial legislatures and the federal and provincial executives could simply create bodies distinct from themselves, vest those bodies with the power to perform governmental functions and, thereby, avoid the constraints imposed upon their activities through the operation of the Charter.
>
> Clearly, this course of action would indirectly narrow the ambit [scope] of protection afforded by the Charter in a manner that could hardly have been intended and with consequences that are, to say the least, undesirable. Indeed, in view of their fundamental importance, *Charter rights must be*

safeguarded from possible attempts to narrow their scope unduly or to circumvent altogether the obligations they engender [emphasis added].

Yet, having said this, the fact remains that if the entity in question is not performing government functions, it will not be covered by the Charter. In the bus case, the Court stated:

Thus, there are two ways to determine whether the Charter applies to an entity's activities: by enquiring into the nature of the entity or by enquiring into the nature of its activities. If the entity is found to be "government," either because of its very nature or because the government exercises substantial control over it, all its activities will be subject to the Charter. If an entity is not itself a government entity but nevertheless performs governmental activities, only those activities which can be said to be governmental in nature will be subject to the Charter.

TECHNOLOGY: NEW CHOICE?

Question: Should courts consider alternatives when claims are made that public forums have been blocked to those who want to exercise their right to free expression? In this regard, should the courts be open to the development of new technology as a channel for expression?
Answer: Yes, to both questions. In the bus case, the Supreme Court of Canada stated that the case was not one in which the Court had to decide whether to protect access to a space where the government entity had never before recognized a right to such access. Rather, the question was whether the side of a bus, as a public place where expressive activity is already occurring, is a location where constitutional protection for free expression would be expected.

Justice Deschamps stated:

> I do not see any aspect of the location that suggests
> that expression within it would undermine the val-
> ues underlying free expression. On the contrary,
> the space allows for expression by a broad range of
> speakers to a large public audience and expression
> there could actually further the values underlying
> section 2(b) of the Charter. I therefore conclude
> that the side of a bus is a location where expressive
> activity is protected by section 2(b) of the Charter.
>   Consequently, I conclude that since the tran-
> sit authorities' policies limit the respondents' right
> to freedom of expression under section 2(b), the
> government must justify that limit under section
> 1 of the Charter.

(Note: Generally, the Court will consider only those matters that have been brought before it. There is nothing in the bus case to indicate that the Court was briefed on the use of the Internet as an alternative forum to that of a bus. Of course, it is always possible for the Court, once it receives briefs from the parties, or even after oral arguments before the Court, to request further written submissions. Again, however, there is nothing to indicate that such submissions were sought in relation to the "new technology of the internet.")

CONSUMER REVENGE: "UNITED BREAKS GUITARS"

Until July 2009, Dave Carroll, a young Canadian musician, leader of a small band (with three others, including his brother, Don) known as the Sons of Maxwell, could not be called a celebrity. But, he had "gigs" that brought him to different parts of Canada and the

United States. That month, the band had been playing in Halifax, Nova Scotia. They were then scheduled to play in Nebraska. They took a plane from Halifax to Chicago's O'Hare Airport. From there they were to fly United Airlines to Nebraska.

From his passenger window in Chicago, Carroll saw United Airlines ground employees treating his $3,500 Taylor custom acoustic guitar roughly. When he collected the guitar in Nebraska, he discovered it had been damaged. He informed United employees, both in Chicago and later in Nebraska, of what he had seen. The response: There was nothing they could do.

Carroll did not let the complaint end. For nine months, he tried to get United to acknowledge responsibility. His goal was not a financial settlement. Rather, his goal became of one getting a major carrier to be more sensitive to customer complaints.

A DIFFERENT TACK

At the end of the year, Carroll took another approach. He asked himself: "What would Michael Moore do?" His response was to use his talent to reach the airline. He wrote a song he titled "United Breaks Guitars." It was an entertaining country-western tune that told the story of what had happened to his guitar.

Carroll posted a performance of the song on YouTube. It was referenced on Twitter, and noted on Carroll's blog with a brief statement of the events that led to its composition. The refrain of the song, in part, goes: "United breaks guitars.... You broke it, you should fix it."

On its first day of posting, 154,301 persons viewed the video. Within a few more days, the number increased to 221,882. And, a few weeks later, the number climbed to 3,442,616. Because of the reach of the Internet, the song was heard around the world. CNN gave it two minutes of viewing time. And, it was screened on CBC and CTV national news in Canada.

One comment, seemingly typical, stated: "On behalf of all musicians who have suffered similar experiences at the hands of airline employees, thanks for posting this great video. It definitely struck a chord with me (pun intended)."

United soon was on the phone with Carroll. The airline wanted to "make things right." Carroll made it clear that he didn't want any money. But, he did agree that United make a contribution to a charity of the airline's choosing so long as he was informed who received it.

United also made it clear that it intended to use the video for "training purposes." It provided a "learning opportunity" for the airline.

THE POINT

Carroll, like the B.C. students and teachers, had a message directed toward a large audience. The students and the teachers wanted people to turn out the vote on election day. In part, their means was advertising on bus side panels. Carroll wanted to reach actual and potential customers of United Airlines with a view toward getting the airline to rethink its approach to customer complaints.

On the face of it, the relative costs were significantly different: If the students and teachers persisted in bus advertising, they would have to pay — just as any advertiser. And the costs presumably would be substantial. Carroll had minimal costs. He did not have to pay Twitter or YouTube, as such. This is not to say that there weren't expenses in the making of the video. But, there were no expenses for the broadcast of the video.

GRAFFITI OR ART? THE ARTIST BROUGHT TO ACCOUNT

Shepard Fairey, an American born in 1970, creates what some describe as guerilla-style art and others describe as graffiti. In 2008 his poster entitled *Hope* — an art poster rendering of Barack Obama — became symbolic of the presidential campaign that brought Obama to office.

Fairey is known for clambering over fences and scaling walls to paint or otherwise render his (what some call) "propagandistic" art — simple, strong pictures. He often does not seek permission from the owners of property on which his art appears. And, often the owners of the property subject to Fairey's art have sought police assistance.

By 2009 Fairey had been arrested fourteen times. He was usually charged with a misdemeanor, among the least serious of crimes, the record of which is erased after six months. He usually pleaded guilty and paid a fine.

In July 2009 Fairey pleaded guilty to three vandalism charges in Boston (one charge of defacing property and two charges of wanton destruction of property) as part of a plea bargain that saw prosecutors drop eleven other vandalism charges. The judge sentenced Fairey to two years of probation, a fine of $250, and an order to pay $2,000 to a graffiti removal organization.

(It may be asked whether Fairey must "struggle" to pay such fines. The answer is probably *no* at this stage in his career. Individual works of his art have now brought him as much as $85,000, and studio signed prints $20,000. However, climbing fences and scaling walls may affect his health. He suffers from diabetes, and wears an insulin drip pack under his shirt.)

ART AND "STREET ART" CONVERGE

The acts that led to vandalism charges in Boston occurred as Fairey was taking part in an art exhibition of his work in the city. Jill Medvedow, Boston Director of the Institute of Contemporary Art (ICA), said of Fairey: "He's raising important issues about consent and who decides what we see in public places.... It gives Boston an opportunity not just to engage but to help lead that debate."

The ICA was happy that Fairey's legal issues with the Boston Police had been resolved and that the focus could now return to where it belonged: on his artistic accomplishments, his outstanding exhibition at the ICA, and the meaningful contributions he had made to the visual and political culture of his country.

Fairey's exhibition, titled *Supply and Demand,* included a retrospective of more than 250 works. He had been named "Icon Maker of the Year" by *Time* magazine. His ubiquitous *Hope* poster became an iconic image of Obama's presidential campaign.

The retrospective, the first solo museum show for the street artist, explored the breadth of Fairey's artistic practice — from screen prints of political revolutionaries and rock stars, to recent mixed-media works and a new mural commissioned for the ICA show.

More than one hundred thousand people saw the Fairey showing — the highest number of visitors for a single exhibition since the opening of the ICA's new building on the Boston waterfront. The exhibition then moved to the Andy Warhol Museum in Pittsburgh, and from there to the Contemporary Arts Center in Cincinnati.

YOU BE THE JUDGE

THE BAND COMES TO TOWN

THE FACTS

Kenneth Ramsden's band had two "gigs" scheduled in the City of Peterborough, Ontario. His audience would be drawn largely from city residents. It seemed to him that a good way to publicize the event and attract an audience was to place posters on hydro poles on public land. Glue was used to fasten the posters to hydro poles for each event.

City officials, however, did not want the postering. A city by-law, not unlike that of many other municipalities, had been enacted concerning postering. The by-law stated:

> No bill, poster, sign or other advertisement of any nature whatsoever shall be placed on or caused to be placed on any public property or placed on or attached to or caused to be placed or attached to any tree situated on any public property within the limits of the City of Peterborough or on any pole, post, stanchion or other object which is used for the purpose of carrying the transmission lines of any telephone, telegraph or electric power company situated on any public property within the limits of the City of Peterborough.
>
> Every person who contravenes this by-law is guilty of an offence and liable upon summary conviction to a penalty not to exceed two thousand dollars

($2,000.00) exclusive of costs for each and
every such offence.

Ramsden was charged twice under the by-law. He was
brought before a justice of the peace, and he was found guilty
and fined. His constitutional argument that his right to freedom of expression had been violated was rejected by the court.

The parties, however, agreed that "postering on utility
poles can constitute a safety hazard to workers climbing
them and a traffic hazard if placed facing traffic." They also
agreed that "abandoned posters or those left for an unreasonable length of time may constitute visual and aesthetic
blight and contribute to litter."

Ramsden's appeal to the Provincial Court was dismissed.
His further appeal to the Court of Appeal was allowed by a
majority of the members of the court who found that the
by-law infringed on his freedom of expression and was not jus-
tifiable under section 1 of the Charter. Accordingly, Ramsden's
convictions were set aside and acquittals were entered.

THE ISSUE

Under the Charter, was the by-law lawful?

POINTS TO CONSIDER

- The event Ramsden postered was a for-profit
  venture. It was not a charitable event.
- The Charter is part of the Constitution of Canada.
  As such, all laws must conform to the Charter.

- Section 2(b) of the Charter provides: "Everyone has the following fundamental freedoms: ... freedom of thought, belief, opinion and expression, including freedom of the press and other media of communication."
- Section 1 of the Charter provides: "The Canadian Charter of Rights and Freedoms guarantees the rights and freedoms set out in it subject only to such reasonable limits pre-scribed by law as can be demonstrably justified in a free and democratic society."

DISCUSSION

The Supreme Court of Canada ruled the city by-law uncon-stitutional. It was a violation of section 2(b) of the Charter that could not otherwise be sustained under section 1 of the Charter as a "reasonable limit prescribed by law as can be justified in a free and democratic society." Justice Frank Iacobucci handed down the Court's unanimous decision in *Ramsden v. Peterborough (City)*, [1993] 2 *Supreme Court of Canada Reports* 1084.

IS POSTERING "EXPRESSION"?
The start point in the Court's analysis was to ask:

1. Was postering the hydro poles "expression" within the meaning of section 2(b) of the Charter? And, in that regard, did it convey meaning?

    If the answer is *yes*, then Ramsden would have

made out a *prima facie* (that is, initial) case that his section 2(b) right to freedom of expression had been violated. It was his burden to prove the *prima facie* violation. Then, if he did so, the burden would shift to the city to prove that it was justified in limiting Ramsden's freedom of expression within the meaning of section 1 of the Charter.

On the face of it, the answer must be *yes*. The postering, said the Court, was an effective and relatively inexpensive way to inform those who read the poster of the band's coming events. The Court concluded: "Regardless of whether the posters concerned constitute advertising, political speech or art, it is clear that they convey a meaning. Therefore, the first part of the section 2(b) test is satisfied."

Ramsden had not simply placed graffiti on the hydro poles.

2. Is commercial postering protected by section 2(b) of the Charter?

Although Ramsden's messages were commercial, Justice Iacobucci said that they served a social purpose. They were a way to communicate. He quoted from the testimony of art historian Robert Stacey, author of *The Canadian Poster Book: 100 Years of the Poster in Canada,* in a human rights matter:

> [Mr. Stacey] testified it was early recognized that posters were an effective and inexpensive way of reaching a large number of persons. In order to be effective, posters of course must be affixed to a surface and publicly displayed. Posters are traditionally

used by minority groups to publicize new ideas or causes. Posters are both a political weapon and an educational device.

According to Mr. Stacey, one measure of the openness of a democratic society has been the willingness of the authorities to allow postering.... Posters are an economic way of spreading a message. Utility poles have become the preferred postering place since the inception of the telephone system....

Posters have always been a medium of communication of revolutionary and unpopular ideas. They have been called "the circulating libraries of the poor." They have been not only a political weapon but also a means of communicating artistic, cultural and commercial messages. Their modern day use for effectively and economically conveying a message testifies to their venerability through the ages.

I would adopt this characterization of the relationship between the message and the forum in the present case. In my view, it is clear that postering on public property, including utility poles, fosters political and social decision-making and thereby furthers at least one of the values underlying section 2(b)....

It is clear that the effect of the by-law is to limit expression. The absolute prohibition of postering on public property prevents the communication of political, cultural and artistic messages. The [City of Peterborough] did not dispute that the effect of the by-law is to restrict expression, but rather argued that postering on public property does not further any of the values underlying section 2(b). As I have already concluded, the expression in question promotes political and social discourse, one of the underlying purposes of section 2(b). Therefore, the respondent has established a violation of section 2(b), and the analysis now proceeds to section 1.

WAS THE BY-LAW JUSTIFIED UNDER SECTION 1 OF THE CHARTER?

The City of Peterborough still could (and did) argue that the by-law could be saved through section 1 of the Charter. An otherwise unlawful violation of section 2(b) might be ruled lawful if it were a reasonable limit that could be demonstrably justified in a free and democratic society.

Justice Iacobucci examined the purpose of the by-law. He said that it was not intended to censor any particular message. In fact, it was "content-neutral." It was intended to stop all messages delivered in a certain way — by placing them on hydro poles and other public property. By forbidding such postering, the City wanted (a) to avoid litter, and (b) to prevent traffic hazards to persons involved in traffic maintenance and repair.

Justice Iacobucci said there was merit in such legislative goals. And, there was no doubt that the no-postering by-law achieved these ends. But, did that meet the test of section 1?

The answer is *no*. The by-law suffered from the defect

of overkill. Bear in mind that section 1 of the Charter is a defence to a violation of a fundamental freedom — freedom of expression. The exceptions are to be read narrowly to allow as much of the impinged freedom as possible to survive. Justice Iacobucci stated:

> The question therefore becomes whether the by-law restricts expression as little as is reasonably possible. The limitation at issue in the present case is a complete ban on postering on public property.... With regard to the objectives identified by the appellant in the present case, worker safety is only affected with respect to posters attached to wooden utility poles. The by-law extends to trees, all types of poles, and all other public property. Traffic safety is only affected where posters are displayed facing roadways. The application of the by-law is not so restricted.

WHAT COULD HAVE BEEN DONE?

Question: Was it possible for the City to have a by-law which could have achieved the values Justice Iacobucci found valid under the Charter — that would have permitted postering and, at the same time, eliminated littering and prevention of traffic hazards?
Answer: *Yes.* Justice Iacobucci referred to another case where the court spelled out what a more precise anti-postering by-law could allow:

> Such values might equally be preserved by regulating the use of the poles for such purposes by

specifying or regulating the location, the size of posters, the length of time that a poster might remain in any location, the type of substance used to affix posters, and requiring that the posters be removed after a certain specified time. If necessary, a reasonable fee could be imposed to defray costs of administering such a system....

These kinds of alternatives could control the concerns of litter and aesthetic blight in a manner which is far less restrictive than the by-law. In my view, the total ban on postering on public property does not impair the right as little as is reasonably possible, given the many alternatives available to the [City].

YOU BE THE JUDGE

TOBACCO: A BAN ON ADVERTISING AND PROMOTION

You probably know the outcome of this case. However, what may not be so clear are the issues and the reasoning that brought the Supreme Court of Canada to its decision. And, those matters really are what drive court decision-making. They allow us to understand more readily how courts, and especially the Supreme Court of Canada, reach decisions.

THE FACTS

The case is a challenge by the tobacco industry against a wide range of legislative prohibitions of advertising and promotional tobacco consumer practices. The legislation with which we are concerned is included in the Tobacco Act of 1997 (*Statutes of Canada*, chapter 13). The case pitted tobacco manufacturers against the Attorney General of Canada, who was supported by a number of provincial attorneys general and the Canadian Cancer Society.

The tobacco manufacturers challenged six parts of the law:

1. Its effect on funded scientific publications;
2. provisions dealing with false, deceptive and erroneous promotion;
3. advertising appealing to young persons;
4. prohibition of "lifestyle" advertising;
5. a ban on sponsorship promotion; and
6. requiring health warning labels on much of tobacco packaging.

Significant evidence was presented in Parliamentary hearings in support of the then-proposed law. But, in the final analysis, that evidence would not be binding on the Supreme Court because it was not subject to challenge by way of cross examination and the presentation of contrary evidence.

The constitutionality of the Tobacco Act was challenged. In support of the law, the government presented to the trial court detailed evidence that the limits on free expression were, in the words of section 1 of the Charter, demonstrably justified. The trial judge found: "Tobacco is now irrefutably accepted as highly addictive and as imposing huge personal and social costs. We now know that half of smokers will die of tobacco-related diseases and that the costs to the public health system are enormous. We also know that tobacco addiction is one of the hardest addictions to conquer and that many addicts try to quit time and time again, only to relapse."

Still, the tobacco companies argued against the constitutionality of the Tobacco Act. For our purposes, we will deal only with the Tobacco Act's advertising limits on lifestyle promotions and sponsorship.

THE ISSUE

Are the limits placed on such advertising valid under the Charter?

POINTS TO CONSIDER

- Section 2(b) of the Charter provides as a fundamental right freedom of expression.
- This right applies to commercial statements, including advertising, so long as it fits within those social values deemed covered by the Charter.
- There is no question that the Tobacco Act does violate the section 2(b) right of the tobacco companies.
- However, government may override the right to freedom of expression if such action comes as a result of law and it can be seen as demonstrably justified in a free and democratic society. Such is the thrust of section 1 of the Charter.
- The government has the burden of proving that its actions in banning or otherwise modifying

tobacco advertising is justified under section 1 of the Charter.

- As part of the government's burden, it must prove that the law challenged is reasonably related to a wrong sought to be remedied — that it is, in effect, proportional.

DISCUSSION

The Supreme Court of Canada, in a unanimous decision handed down by Chief Justice McLachlin, upheld the Tobacco Act. The case was *Attorney General of Canada v. JTI-Macdonald Corp.*, [2007] 2 *Supreme Court of Canada Reports* 610.

We will address two of the more important issues raised in the appeal to the Supreme Court — first by describing them in somewhat more detail, and then giving the Court's reasoning for sustaining the applicable law. Bear in mind that the tobacco companies argued that an important reason for striking these provision was their vagueness.

1. Lifestyle advertising is defined broadly under the Tobacco Act. It means "advertising that associates a product with, or evokes a positive or negative emotion about or image of, a way of life such as one that includes glamour, recreation, excitement, vitality, risk or daring."

2. Sponsorship ban, under the Tobacco Act, means that tobacco manufacturers are not permitted to use their brand elements or names to sponsor events, nor to put those brand elements or names on sports or cultural facilities. (Not included in the ban, contrary to

arguments made by the tobacco manufacturers, is the right to sponsor sporting or cultural events without the use of their name or brand attribution. In effect, they could become unknown givers.)

The companies said that the law, as interpreted by the attorney general, was difficult to understand. It simply was not clear what practices were intended to be deemed unlawful. And, if the practices were not clear, then how could it be said that Parliament intended to only impose the minimum amount of sanctions necessary to remedy the wrong found? Or, as the Supreme Court had earlier ruled, the restraint on free expression must be proportional — a balance between the wrong to be remedied and the means chosen to effect that end.

THE TASK OF THE DECISION-MAKER

The language of the Tobacco Act, on its face, was by no means clear. In part, the reason reflected the difficulty of Parliament to come to grips with claims and advertisements that could slip by the intent of public policy. Parliament wanted to ensure a means for bringing tobacco claims now and in the future to account — to ensure that neither claims of health nor promotional pitches, especially to the young, would be tolerated. So, the Court read the legislative language in a way that was proportional. This is what the chief justice said in part:

> Parliament ... was concerned with emotions and images that may induce people to start to use or to increase their use of tobacco. Parliament used these terms in the context of its purpose — to prevent

the increase of tobacco consumption through advertising and to confine permissible advertising to hard, factual data directed to confirmed smokers. The provision should be construed accordingly.

The reference to "positive or negative" emotion poses a further difficulty (both of which were condemned in the Tobacco Act). One would expect lifestyle advertising to evoke a positive emotion about the lifestyle and the use of the product. However, it is not beyond the ingenuity of advertisers to rely on negative emotions to subtly persuade. A lifestyle depiction that sends messages of non-smokers being left out of the crowd or being seen as unsophisticated comes to mind.

And, what is the effect of qualifying "way of life" in [the Tobacco Act] with the words "such as one that includes glamour, recreation, excitement, vitality, risk or daring"? The words "such as" indicate that "way of life" is not limited by the terms that follow. Rather, they are to be read as illustrations of lifestyle advertising....

Read in this way, the prohibition on lifestyle advertising is reasonable and demonstrably justified under section 1 of the Charter. As with the other challenged provisions, the pressing and substantial nature of Parliament's objective is beyond challenge.

The record is replete with examples of lifestyle advertisements promoting tobacco products. It amply establishes the power of such advertisements to induce non-smokers to begin to smoke, and to increase tobacco consumption among addicted smokers. It also establishes the sophistication and subtlety of such advertising. Lifestyle advertising spans the spectrum from the bold association of the Marlboro man with cowboy culture to the subtle suggestion emerging from a cup of coffee or a bath scene that evokes tobacco use through learned prior imagery.

The sophistication and subtlety of lifestyle advertising are reflected in the means Parliament has chosen to deal with it. A ban on lifestyle advertising must catch not only clear associations, but subtle subliminal evocations. Hence the inclusion of advertising that "evokes a positive or negative emotion or image." There is a rational connection between this provision and Parliament's objective. Minimal impairment is also established.

True information and brand-preference advertising continues to be permitted under [the Tobacco Act]. Such advertising crosses the line when it associates a product with a way of life or uses a lifestyle to evoke an emotion or image that may, by design or effect, lead more people to become addicted or lead people who are already addicted to increase their tobacco use. Finally, the proportionality of the effects is clear. The suppressed expression — the inducement of increased tobacco consumption — is of low value, compared with the significant benefits in lower rates of consumption and addiction that the ban may yield.

The challenge of dealing with today's sophisticated advertising of tobacco products is not insignificant. The distinction between information and brand-preference advertising directed to market share, on the one hand, and advertising directed to increased consumption and new smokers, on the other, is difficult to capture in legal terms. Parliament in its wisdom has chosen to take the task on. Properly interpreted, the law it has adopted meets the requirements of justification under section 1 of the Charter.

SPONSORSHIPS

Yet, what can be said of sponsorships? Isn't the reality that sponsorships are just another kind of lifestyle advertising? For example, isn't sponsorship by cigarette manufacturers of tennis tournaments just another way of inferring that tennis, a vigorous life, and smoking go together? If so, what is the need for additional legislation relating to a ban on sponsorships? This is what the chief justice, speaking for a unanimous Court, stated:

Tobacco manufacturers have a long tradition of sponsoring sporting and cultural events and facilities as a means of promoting their product and, they would argue, acting as good corporate citizens. Parliament, in the Tobacco Act, has chosen to ban the promotion of these sponsorships. The question is whether that ban is constitutional.

Section 24 of the [Tobacco Act] bans the display of tobacco-related brand elements or names in promotions that are used, directly or indirectly, in the "sponsorship of a person, entity, event, activity or permanent facility." Section 25 goes further and prohibits the display of tobacco-related brand elements or names on a permanent facility, if the brand elements or names are thereby associated with a sports or cultural event or activity. Together, these sections mean that tobacco manufacturers are not permitted to use their brand elements or names to sponsor events, nor to put those brand elements or names on sports or cultural facilities.

Two questions arise. The first is whether the general ban on sponsorship is constitutional. Since it clearly limits freedom of expression under section 2(b) of the Charter, the only issue is whether it has been shown to be justified under section 1 of the Charter. The Supreme Court stated:

The prohibition of sponsorship promotion is rationally connected to the legislative goal for the same reasons as for the prohibition on lifestyle advertising. Similarly, since the ban on lifestyle advertising is accepted as minimally impairing, so is the ban on sponsorship. A finding of minimal impairment is reinforced by the fact that Parliament phased in the ban over five years so that it would not have a disruptive impact. I would also note that, contrary to their assertions, the manufacturers are not prohibited from sponsoring anything; they are only prohibited from using the fact of their sponsorship to gain publicity.

The second question, the use of corporate names in sponsorship, is more complicated. The Supreme Court stated:

Parliament's objective, once again, is clearly pressing and substantial.... The evidence establishes that as restrictions on tobacco advertising tightened, manufacturers increasingly turned to sports and cultural sponsorship as a substitute form of lifestyle promotion. Placing a tobacco manufacturer's name on a facility is one form such sponsorship takes. The prohibition on sponsorship by means of names on facilities in section 25 only applies to facilities used for sports or cultural activities, not for all facilities. The aim of curbing such promotion justifies imposing limits on free expression.

Nor is the means chosen to achieve the objective disproportionate. The element of rational connection is made out. Placing a corporate name on a list of sponsors or on a sports or cultural facility may promote the use of tobacco in a number of ways. This is clear when the corporate name is connected with the brand name of a tobacco product.... But even where there is no [stated] connection between the corporate name and the brand name of a tobacco product, the corporate name may serve to promote the sale of the tobacco product.

Connections may be established in a variety of ways. The corporate name may, without referencing a brand name, nevertheless contain a reference to tobacco. Or the corporate name may have historically been associated with tobacco. The evidence established the tobacco industry's practice of using shell corporations as an element in brand identification. Associations between the parent company and the shell company may persist in the public mind. As a result, the corporate name in the sponsorship promotion or on the building or facility may evoke a connection with the shell company and its brand.

Given the nature of the problem, and in view of the limited value of the expression in issue compared with the beneficial effects of the ban, the proposed solution

— a total ban on the use of corporate names in sponsorship promotion, or on sports or cultural facilities — is proportional. And in view of the limited value of the expression in issue compared with the beneficial effects of the ban, proportionality of effects is established.... I conclude that the impugned sponsorship provisions are a reasonable limit justified under section 1 of the Charter.

BACKGROUND TO THE TOBACCO ACT: SECOND TIME AROUND

The Tobacco Act was not the first time Parliament tried to regulate advertising and sales practices of tobacco companies. Only two years before the Tobacco Act, the Supreme Court of Canada was called upon to review similar legislation, which it struck down as unconstitutional — a violation of the Charter right to freedom of expression under section 2(b).

The new act, the Tobacco Act, was an attempt to remedy the defects of the old law. This was done, in no small measure, based on a kind of template laid out by the Supreme Court of Canada in its earlier rulings. And, it was done, in part, based on Parliamentary hearings and lower court findings of fact which were quite detailed as to the health hazards of tobacco use. As well, there were differences in the new law compared to the old law.

The Supreme Court of Canada set out the background for the Tobacco Act in the second time around. It stated:

Before analyzing the six disputed aspects of the legislative and regulatory scheme, it is necessary to set the stage by discussing the historical background of the legislation and its social and legal contexts.

In 1995, this Court struck down the advertising provisions of the Tobacco Products Control Act (*Statutes of Canada 1988*, chapter 20): *RJR-MacDonald Inc. v. Canada (Attorney General)*, [1995] 3 *Supreme Court of Canada Reports* 199. This Act broadly prohibited all advertising and promotion of tobacco products, subject to specific exceptions, and required affixing unattributed warning labels on tobacco product packaging.

The majority of the Court in that case held that the provisions limited free expression and that the government had failed to justify the limitations under section 1 of the Charter. In particular, the government, by failing to show that less intrusive measures were not available, had failed to establish that the limits met the requirement of minimal impairment developed in *The Queen v. Oakes*, [1986] 1 *Supreme Court of Canada Reports* 103 (McLachlin J., at paras. 163 and 165, and Iacobucci J., at para. 191). While the majority agreed that section 1 justification on issues such as this does not require scientifically precise proof, it found that the absence of virtually any proof was fatal to the government's case. The trial judge had found that the requirements for justification were not met on the evidence. The majority concluded that on the record before it, there was no basis to interfere with the trial judge's conclusion.

In response to the Court's decision in *RJR*, Parliament enacted the Tobacco Act and Regulations at issue on these appeals. The scheme of the new legislation, in broad terms, involved permitting information and brand-preference advertising, while forbidding lifestyle advertising and promotion, advertising appealing to young persons, and false or misleading advertising or promotion. In addition, the size of mandatory and attributed health warnings on packaging was increased from 33 percent to 50 percent of the principal display surfaces. In general, the new scheme was more restrained and nuanced than its predecessor. It represented a genuine attempt by Parliament to craft controls on advertising and promotion that would meet its objectives as well as the concerns expressed by the majority of this Court in *RJR*.

The government's response to the inevitable challenge to the new scheme, when it came, also reflected the Court's decision in *RJR*. The government presented detailed and copious evidence in support of its contention that where the new legislation posed limits on free expression, those limits were demonstrably justified under section 1 of the Charter.

Parliament was assisted in its efforts to craft and justify appropriately tailored controls on tobacco advertising and promotion by increased understanding of the means by which tobacco manufacturers seek to advertise and promote their products and by new scientific insights into the nature of tobacco addiction and its consequences. On the findings of the trial judge in the present case, tobacco is now irrefutably accepted as highly addictive and as imposing huge personal and social costs. We now know that half of smokers will die of tobacco-related diseases and that the costs to the public health system are enormous. We also know that tobacco addiction is one of the hardest addictions to conquer and that many addicts try to quit time and time again, only to relapse.

Moreover, the international context has changed since 1995. Governments around the world are implementing anti-tobacco measures similar to and, in some cases, more restrictive than Canada's. The *WHO Framework Convention on Tobacco Control* (2003), 2302 U.N.T.S. 229, which Canada ratified in 2004, mandates a comprehensive ban on tobacco promotion, subject to state constitutional requirements. The Convention, with 168 signatories and 148 parties, is one of the most widely embraced of multilateral treaties. Domestically, governments now widely accept that protecting the public from second-hand smoke is a legitimate policy objective. Many provinces have banned smoking in enclosed public places, and some are legislating to recover health care costs from tobacco manufacturers and to restrict tobacco promotion even further than the federal Tobacco Act. The tobacco industry has been criticized for its use of light and mild cigarette designations, which the manufacturers agreed in 2006 to discontinue following an investigation by the Competition Bureau.

None of these developments remove the burden on the Crown to show that limitations on free expression imposed by the legislation are demonstrably justified in a free and democratic society, as required by section 1 of the Charter. The mere fact that the legislation represents Parliament's response to a decision of this Court does not militate for or against deference.... The legal template set out in *Oakes* and *RJR* remains applicable. However, when that template is applied to the evidence adduced by the government in this case more than a decade later, different conclusions may emerge. *RJR* was grounded in a different historical context and based on different findings supported by a different record at a different time. The Tobacco Act must be assessed in light of the knowledge, social conditions and regulatory environment revealed by the evidence presented in this case.

THE QUESTIONS CONTINUE

Tobacco companies have put resources into packaging. A study led by David Hammond, a professor of health studies at the University of Waterloo, Ontario found that cigarette packaging, itself, may influence consumer perceptions. For example, the lighter the packaging bearing words like "smooth" and "filter," the more likely consumers are to identify the cigarettes contained with fewer health hazards. The study was conducted in Ontario and involved six hundred adults.

Professor Hammond said: "Cigarette packaging is associated with false beliefs about the risks of cigarettes and obviously that's a problem.... The pack is now the most important marketing tool in Canada."

REFERENCES AND FURTHER READING
* Cited by the Supreme Court of Canada.

Barak, Aharon. 2007. "Proportional Effect: The Israeli Experience." *University of Toronto Law Journal* 57:369.*

Cameron, Jamie B. 1992. "A Bumpy Landing: The Supreme Court of Canada and Access to Public Airports under Section 2(b) of the Charter." *Media & Communications Law Review* 2: 91.*

Daily Kos. "Obama Poster Artist Shepard Fairey Cops Plea, Sentenced to Probation." July 14, 2009.

Globe and Mail. "Captives of Democracy." July 11, 2009.

Hogg, Peter W., Allison A. Bushell Thornton and Wade K. Wright. 2007. "Charter Dialogue Revisited — Or 'Much Ado About Metaphors.'" *Osgoode Hall Law Journal* 45: 1.*

Kanter, Michael. 1992. "Balancing Rights under Section 2(b) of the Charter: Case Comment on Committee for the Commonwealth of Canada v. Canada." *Queen's Law Journal* 17: 489.*

Makin, Kirk. "Transit Must Allow Political Ads: Court." *Globe and Mail,* July 11, 2009.

Mehta, Diana. "Snazzy Cigarette Packaging Has Consumers Thinking the Product Is Less Lethal." *The Record,* July 28, 2009.

New York Times "Shepard Fairey." March 12, 2009.

Stacey, Robert. 1979. *The Canadian Poster Book: 100 Years of the Poster in Canada.* Toronto: Methuen Publishers.

Stelter, Brian. "*Time* Cover Sure Looks a Lot Like a Campaign Image." *New York Times,* December 21, 2008.

2

CHAPTER 2
HATE: A PRIVATE MATTER?

The dictionary defines hate as: "intense hostility and aversion usually derived from fear, anger, sense of injury." In this chapter, our focus is on how the law treats hate — especially in the context of the Charter right to freedom of expression. Here it is important to bear in mind some of the limits of law. Law is an expression of public policy establishing defined rights and punishing defined wrongs. How does this apply to hate?

One can hate alone, and the law does not forbid this. (After all, how could the law objectively probe and prove the inner working of the mind?) Nor does law prohibit hate expressed to another in private conversation. Nor does law prevent the opinion of hate directed against an individual, as such, even though that opinion is broadly expressed. (However, making that expression a statement of fact, publicly stated, that is false and harms the person attacked may be a basis for an individual action in libel or slander by the person harmed.)

To say that an individual may have the legal right to hate, and under certain circumstances to even express and act upon such hate, is not to put a stamp of state approval on such action. After all, the state is not the only force in society. There are other powerful societal moral forces, like religion. In a number of ways, for example, Christianity and Judaism both strike at hate through the expression of the "Golden Rule." Do unto others what you would have them do unto you. And, do not do unto others what you would not have them do unto you.

Among the questions raised in this chapter are:

- Does the law control expressions of hate?
- Does it matter whether such expressions are directed against an individual or a group?
- In law, are opinions treated differently than statements of fact?
- What is the role of deportation (forced removal from the state) for those who incite hate?

The law, among other things, does set limits on the intentional expression of hate publicly stated against any "identifiable group." Here the expression is a communication carried to the public. And, the attack is not just against an individual, but it is against a group. Indeed, the communication may not even mention an individual's name. It may be an attack against a race, or a religion, or those of a particular ethnic group.

The law against hate is legislation under the Criminal Code and/ or the human rights codes of the federal government and the provinces. And, the law does not end with targeted expressions of hate against identifiable groups. Parliament has recognized that public expressions of hate may give rise to calls for violence, and even result in violence itself directed against individuals, such as hate-inspired assault, and in action designed to undermine the state itself.

The language and action of hate against groups, in turn, may impact on public security — on peace, order, and good government. When such threats occur, they may be perceived as a danger to national security. To meet such challenges, Canada (like many other nations, especially since the terrorist bombings in the United States on September 11, 2001) has enacted heightened criminal restrictions that have been applied to those who have used hate to threaten the country's security. Examples of such hate include intimidating minorities from freely enjoying their rights as citizens, or even urging public unrest to undermine the government in the pursuit of goals such as "white supremacy."

Human rights codes and criminal laws are statutes created by the legislatures. They can be changed (strengthened or weakened) generally as the legislatures see fit. In a democracy, these law-making bodies are voices of democracy. In Canada, human rights codes are used to further equality and to promote human dignity by preventing discrimination against individuals and identifiable groups. In human rights codes, punishment is not the end sought for violations. Rather, remedies are imposed to correct what has been found unlawful. However, the criminal law is used to punish actions resulting in hate crimes and hate propaganda.

In this chapter, we will examine cases involving the criminal law, as well as one involving national security applied to the deportation of a Canadian resident who was returned to his native Germany, there to face a hate crime that falls outside the net of Canadian hate offences. Ordinarily, criminal laws are interpreted narrowly. The reason: they can result in punishment, including imprisonment, and a loss of individual freedom. But, when those laws relate to hate, we tend to see them given a broad, or purposive interpretation. The reason: they are intended to foster the important value of human dignity.

These very laws, however, must conform with the Charter of Rights and Freedoms, part of the Constitution of Canada and, as such, the highest law of the nation. Except under rare situations (when, for a limited time, application of the Charter can be suspended by a provincial legislature or Parliament), no statute can conflict with its provisions. Charter freedoms are guarantees against government, not individual, action. And, where there is conflict, it is to be settled, in the final analysis, by the courts, with final judgment from the Supreme Court of Canada.

(It should be noted that the Supreme Court may point the way that the legislature might remake questioned laws to satisfy Charter demands. Time and again, the Court has noted that it is a co-equal part of government and, if possible, it will suggest, in any specific case, the zone in which a legislature might act to shape acceptable constitutional public policy.)

Key among the Charter provisions, for our purposes, is section 2(b) which provides that "everyone has the following fundamental freedoms … (b) freedom of thought, belief, opinion and expression, including freedom of the press and other media of communication…." The expression and communication of hate certainly falls within the protection of section 2(b). Anti-hate laws are government action directed against individual expression. Are such laws, in and of themselves, not violations of the Charter? The answer is *yes*. If so, are they not then unconstitutional and thus invalid?

The answer is *not necessarily*. The reason: The Charter has another relevant provision that conditions the application of section 2(b). Section 1 provides: "The Canadian Charter of Rights and Freedoms guarantees the rights and freedoms set out in it [such as section 2(b) — freedom of expression] subject only to such reasonable limits prescribed by law as can be demonstrably justified in a free and democratic society."

An anti-hate law can be constitutional if, in the words of section 1 of the Charter, it is a "reasonable limit" set by law which can be "demonstrably justified in a free and democratic society." Among other things, to pass constitutional muster, such a law must be designed to realistically meet a legitimate government objective in the context of a free and democratic society. Valid government objectives could be seen as protecting citizen rights to equality, for example, and preventing such actions as might undermine democratic government institutions.

This chapter centres on two cases, one decided by the Supreme Court of Canada and the other an opinion of the Federal Court of Canada: *The Queen v. Krystopher Krymowski, Ryan Douglas*

Marshall and others, Supreme Court of Canada, February 24, 2005 (the Roma case), and *In the Matter of Ernst Zundel*, Federal Court of Canada, February 24, 2005 (the Zundel case). Both cases concern the law and expressions of hate.

A MATTER OF INTERPRETATION: THE ROMA CASE

When Canadians think about discrimination against identifiable groups, their thoughts often turn to race, religion, and ethnic or national origin. The Roma case, however, decided by a unanimous Supreme Court of Canada on February 24, 2005, is concerned with the identification of the group against whom attacks were made. The issue was presented under the Criminal Code's anti-hate law (*Revised Statutes of Canada 1985*, chapter C-46). First, we will present the facts of the case and the rulings of the trial and appellate courts, and then the anti-hate law, the decision of the Supreme Court, and background concerning the Roma people.

THE FACTS

The facts that gave rise to the charges against the defendants arose on August 26, 1997. It was more than four years later that the matter reached the Supreme Court, where a decision was handed down — one which we shall see did not result in finding the accused either guilty or innocent of the charges made against them.

On August 26, 1997, according to Justice Louise Charron, who gave the Court's opinion, about twenty-five persons demonstrated in front of the Lido Hotel in Scarborough, Ontario (located in the Greater Toronto Area). At the time, the hotel was being used by government to house a number of Roma refugees as they awaited the outcome of their claims to enter Canada as political refugees.

The demonstrators included several who were juveniles, and others whose clothing and appearance were described in some of the popular press as "typical skinhead." The *Toronto Star* described the demonstration as one of "neo-Nazi skinheads and their supporters" (*Toronto Star,* February 25, 2005).

The demonstrators carried placards displaying messages such as the following: "Honk if you hate gypsies"; "Canada is not a trash can"; "You're a cancer to Canada"; and "G.S.T. — Gypsies Suck Tax." Their chants included such statements as: "Gypsies out"; "White power"; and "How do you like Canada now?" Some of the demonstrators were seen giving the Nazi "Seig Heil" salute, and Nazi and American Confederate flags were in evidence.

The Crown charged six persons (four adults and two juveniles) who, it was claimed, took part in the demonstration and violated Canada's anti-hate law. The trial lasted forty-seven days. The Crown presented its case. But, the defence called no evidence. It argued that the Crown had failed to prove an essential element of the offence charged: *All of the Crown's evidence pointed to statements made allegedly by the accused against gypsies. There was no evidence that linked gypsies to Roma.*

The trial judge agreed with the defence: It was necessary for the Crown to prove that "gypsies" and "Roma" were the same — that they were, in the words of the trial court, "interchangeable terms." The Crown asked for the opportunity to reopen that phase of its case and prove what the judge demanded. The request was refused. In effect, the trial court strictly read the anti-hate law. This was, after all, a criminal law under which an accused, if found guilty, could be imprisoned. One's liberty, a fundamental freedom, could be denied by the state. For that reason, as a general matter, criminal laws are not broadly interpreted.

THE SUPREME COURT DECIDES

The appellate court agreed that the trial judge acted within its authority and that there was no basis for review. The case came before the Supreme Court.

Justice Charron noted the Court's earlier decision in *The Queen v. Keegstra*, [1990] 3 *Supreme Court of Canada Reports* 697, in which the Court upheld the constitutionality of the anti-hate law against claims that it violated the Charter guarantee of freedom of expression. There, the Court said that the law created a defined "narrowly confined offence that suffers from neither overbreadth nor vagueness." The Court stated that to prove the offence requires, in effect, a specific intent to promote hatred, defined as "the most severe and deeply-felt form of opprobrium [contempt]," that is publicly made and focuses on an identifiable group. Justice Charron then summarized the current anti-hate law.

The defence conceded that the Roma are an "identifiable group" within the meaning of the law. As such, the Roma historically had been subject to Nazi persecution, including extermination. Yet, said defence counsel, it remained to be proved that the accused, as part of the demonstration, made the statements challenged. But, more importantly, for purposes of the appeal to the Supreme Court, there was the question as to whether the Roma were the target of the conduct of the accused.

In effect, said Justice Charron for the Court, the trial judge made an important error of law. *It was the sum of all the circumstances of the demonstration that determined whether the anti-hate law had been violated. Whether that law had been violated could not be determined by looking only to whether "Roma" and "gypsies" were interchangeable terms.* She wrote:

> The relevant questions to be asked with respect to this element of the offence were whether the Crown had proved beyond a reasonable doubt that the [accused] made some or all of the statements alleged ... and whether the statements made, as a matter of fact, promoted hatred of the Roma.
>
> It was incumbent upon the trial judge to look at the totality of the evidence and draw

appropriate inferences to determine whether the [accused] intended to target "any section of the public distinguished by colour, race, religion or ethnic origin," in this case, the Roma people. Several items of evidence potentially related to this issue. The reference to "gypsies" was but one item of evidence to consider.

Among other things, the trial judge in his reasons for judgment referred to the following evidence as fact: (1) The motel outside of which the [accused] demonstrated was temporarily housing the refugee claimants who were awaiting the outcome of their claims. (2) Some of the [demonstration] participants were seen giving the "Seig Heil" Nazi salute. (3) Nazi and American Confederate flags were used in the demonstration. And (4) the chant "White power" was heard during the demonstration. Furthermore, the defence concession expressly linked Nazi persecution to the Roma people.

Hence, the ethnic flavour to the demonstration, the fact that it was situated outside a motel housing refugee claimants who were at times described by the witnesses as Roma, and the fact that Roma people are a group historically persecuted by the Nazis while the Nazi theme was apparent at the demonstration, were all factors to consider, in addition to the actual words used, in determining whether Roma were the target of the hate speech. In focussing entirely on one of the specific statements particularized in [the charges made against the accused], the trial judge misdirected himself as to the essential elements of the offence. In doing so, he erred in law.

The Court set aside the acquittals of the accused, and ordered a new trial. Recall that forty-seven days had been used simply to present the Crown's case, and that the defendants offered no evidence. They had relied on the legal claim that the demonstration was directed against gypsies and not Roma. Defence counsel told the media that, if the Crown chose to prosecute again, they would mount a full defence. The Crown, however, decided not to retry the case.

WHY NOT USE THE TERM "GYPSIES"?

Question: If the Crown believed that the terms "Roma" and "gypsies" were in fact interchangeable, why was that not indicated by the prosecution in the charges laid (called the "information")?
Answer: The Ontario Court of Appeal commented on this in the Roma case. It stated that the Crown had destroyed its own case by referring to gypsies as Roma in the hope of not ruffling ethnic sensitivities. The term "gypsy" is seen by many as pejorative, that is, degrading. An estimated 3,000–4,000 Canadians of Roma descent live in the Greater Toronto Area (*Globe and Mail*, February 24, 2005).

THE ANTI-HATE LAW

Section 319 of the Criminal Code sets out the anti-hate law:

§319(2): Every one who, by communicating statements, other than in private conversation, that wilfully promote hatred against any identifiable group is guilty of
    (a) an indictable offence and is liable to imprisonment for a term not exceeding two years; or
    (b) an offence punishable on summary conviction. The term "identifiable group" is defined in §318(4) as meaning any section of the public

distinguished by colour, race, religion or ethnic origin. Certain defences are set out under §319(3) which include the following:

§319(3) No person shall be convicted of an offence under subsection (2)

   (a) if he establishes that the statements communicated were true;

   (b) if, in good faith, he expressed or attempted to establish by argument an opinion on a religious subject;

   (c) if the statements were relevant to any subject of public interest, the discussion of which was for the public benefit, and if on reasonable grounds he believed them to be true; or

   (d) if, in good faith, he intended to point out, for the purpose of removal, matters producing or tending to produce feelings of hatred toward an identifiable group in Canada.

EVIDENCE WITHOUT PROOF?

Question: Was it possible for the Crown to prove that the terms "gypsies" and "Roma" were interchangeable without witness testimony?

Answer: Yes. This is called *judicial notice*. It means that a court may accept without the requirement of proof those facts that are generally accepted "as not to be the subject of debate among reasonable persons," or that are demonstrated by "readily accessible sources of indisputable accuracy."

Justice Charron noted that the Crown presented the trial judge with five dictionaries, all of which showed a relationship between the terms Roma and gypsy. She quoted from the *New Oxford Dictionary of English* (1998), which defined gypsy as "a member of a travelling people with dark skin and hair, speaking a language [Romany] related to Hindi, and traditionally living by seasonal work, itinerant trade, and fortune-telling. Gypsies are now found mostly in Europe, parts of North Africa, and North America, but are believed to have originated in the Indian subcontinent."

Romany was defined as "the language of the gypsies, which is an Indo-European language related to Hindi. It is spoken by a dispersed group of about one million people, and has many dialects."

Justice Charron, speaking for a unanimous Supreme Court, wrote: "The dictionary definitions presented to the trial judge hence showed that 'gypsy' can refer to an ethnic group properly known as 'Roma,' 'Rom,' or 'Romany.' I see no reason why the trial judge should not have taken judicial notice of that fact and then considered it, together with the rest of the evidence, to determine whether there was proof beyond a reasonable doubt that the [accused] did in fact intend to target Roma."

GYPSIES: WHO ARE THEY?

The Roma, along with the closely-related Sinti, are the two largest groups among those who are commonly referred to in English as gypsies. They originated in northern India and now are found mostly in Europe and parts of North Africa, and also in North and South America. (The Sinti are located mainly in northwestern Europe.) They speak a distinct Indo-Iranian language known as Romany.

Traditionally, gypsies were nomads who travelled in groups of households of varying sizes, under the authority of a chief (elected for life). They worked as horse-traders, metal- or basket-workers, wood-carvers, and fortune-tellers. Gypsy music, performed in public exclusively by men, has for many years been highly popular in Central Europe.

Gypsies have often been persecuted, most notably under the Nazis when as many as one-half million are estimated to have perished between 1939 and 1945. Then, postwar communist regimes throughout Eastern Europe forced gypsies to settle in high-rise housing blocks in industrial towns, breaking up extended families and forcing them to work in factories.

Post-communist democratic governments have allowed gypsies to form political parties and to campaign for recognition as an ethnic minority. Associations and pressure groups have been formed to campaign for special schools, and for books in the Romany language. However, the majority still face racial discrimination (especially in Romania), are poorly housed, often unemployed, and often have a lower life expectancy than the rest of the population.

CHALLENGE QUESTION

A DIFFERENT DEMONSTRATION?

Assume the same facts as in the Roma case, with this exception: Neither the placards nor the shouted statements made any mention of gypsies or the Roma. Rather, the thrust of the demonstration was so-called "white power," and the demand was that the immigration door to Canada be closed.

Other features of the demonstration in the Roma case remain. For example, many of the demonstrators appeared to be "skinheads," in terms of their shaved heads and the clothing they wore. They gave the Nazi salute ("Seig Heil"), and carried Nazi and American Confederate flags. They clustered around the motel where the Roma seeking refugee status were housed.

Q: Under the anti-hate law, can it be said that the Roma were a target of the demonstration?

This was a question posed by Justice Charron in the Roma case. She stated: "To illustrate the point, it may be useful to consider whether the offence [violation of the anti-hate law] could be made out even if the demonstrators had made the same statements but without using the word *gypsies*."

The point to which Justice Charron referred — and it is key to the Supreme Court decision in the Roma case — is the *need for a trial court to look to all the evidence to determine whether the accused demonstrators intended to target any section of the public because of their colour, race, religion, or ethnic origin.*

A trial court would have to view the evidence and ask itself if it was reasonable to infer that the demonstrators intended, looking at all the facts, to target the Roma not only as possible immigrants, but as people to be kept out of Canada specifically because of race and/or ethnic origin.

YOU BE THE JUDGE

THE CASE OF "FALSE NEWS"

This case is real. It involves a private prosecution, one where an individual issues a complaint on behalf of the Crown. The individual does not have to prove that she has been directly injured. Rather, she must prove that the law under which she is permitted to bring suit has been violated by the accused.

THE FACTS

Sabina Citron, a Canadian citizen, was a survivor of Nazi Germany's death camps where six million Jews were slaughtered and hundreds of thousands of others, including gypsies, homosexuals, and those deemed mentally retarded, also were murdered during the Second World War. The Nazis claimed this was necessary in order to eliminate so-called undesirables and establish the supremacy of the Aryan and, more particularly, the German "race." The word *Holocaust* has been used to denote this mass murder and, more recently, any mass murder of a group.

Citron urged the Crown to prosecute Ernst Zundel, then head of Samisdat Publishers of Toronto, for violating the "false news" law as set out in section 181 of the Criminal Code: "Everyone who wilfully publishes a statement, tale or news that he knows is false and that causes or is likely to cause injury or mischief to a public interest is guilty of an indictable offence and liable to imprisonment for a term not exceeding two years."

At the heart of Citron's charge was that Zundel was a Holocaust denier, one of a group of so-called "revisionist" historians who said that claims about the Holocaust were part of a worldwide conspiracy to get money from the postwar German government and sympathy for the State of Israel. Initially, the Crown refused to prosecute. But, at a later point, the Crown joined the action against Zundel.

The Crown's case was focussed. It stated that Zundel had published a pamphlet titled *Historical Facts No. 1, Did Six Million Really Die? Truth at Last Exposed.* He had written the preface and afterword. The author of the pamphlet was described as: "Richard Harwood … a writer and specialist in political and diplomatic aspects of the Second World War. At present he is with the University of London." In fact, however, the piece was produced in England in 1977 by Richard Verral, editor of the neo-Nazi British newspaper, *National Front*.

Verral stated why the pamphlet was important. What he

referred to as the "Anglo-Saxon world" was threatened, he said, by the international community's attack against all forms of racism following what has been called the Holocaust. He claimed that many countries, notably Britain and the United States, were then facing the "gravest danger posed by the alien races in their midst." He argued that unless immigration of Africans and Asians to Britain was stopped, racial conflict would result in the destruction of the British people.

Verral questioned what happens "if a man dares to speak of the race problem, of its biological and political implications." He said that the man would be branded as the "most heinous of creatures, a *racialist*."

Verral's argument seemed to be that "racialism," the ethnic "purity" of the Anglo-Saxon race, and the need for "ethnic cleansing" of "impure" races can only be "discussed" if the Holocaust is denied. Otherwise, the universal ethic against racism will assert itself.

THE ISSUES

- Is the knowing denial of the Holocaust a violation of the false news law?
- Is the false news law, itself, unconstitutional as a violation of the Charter of Rights and Freedoms?

POINTS TO CONSIDER

- The false news law can be traced to a law enacted in 1275 by the British Parliament. In 1892, it was placed in the Canadian Criminal Code where it was treated as an offence. In 1887, it was dropped as an offence under British law.

- In 1955, the law ceased to be an offence and instead was treated as a nuisance law (a lesser form of wrongdoing). In the century between 1892 and 1992, the law was used only three times.
- The Holocaust is an issue of historical fact.
- The Charter is part of the Constitution of Canada and, as such, it is the highest law of the land.
- Section 2(b) of the Charter provides: "Everyone has the following fundamental freedoms: ... freedom of thought, belief, opinion and expression, including freedom of the press and other media of communication."
- Section 1 of the Charter provides: "The Canadian Charter of Rights and Freedoms guarantees the rights and freedoms set out in it subject only to such reasonable limits prescribed by law as can be justified in a free and democratic society."

DISCUSSION

Zundel was convicted twice. The first trial, from the laying of charges in 1983 to completion in 1985, brought a sentence of fifteen months imprisonment. The Ontario Court of Appeal set aside the conviction because of errors in the admission of certain evidence. In 1987 it ordered a new trial. The second trial resulted, as noted, in a conviction. This time the court imposed a sentence of nine months imprisonment.

In a constitutional challenge, the Ontario Court of

Appeal unanimously upheld the conviction. The matter came before the Supreme Court of Canada — nine years after the complaint was first filed by the Crown against Zundel. In a 4–3 opinion, then Justice McLachlin, later to become chief justice, declared the false news law unconstitutional, with the result that Zundel's conviction was set aside. (*The Queen v. Zundel*, [1992] 2 *Supreme Court Reports* 731)

THE "FALSE NEWS" LAW: PURPOSE?

Justice McLachlin emphasized that *the complaint was not about spreading hate*. That kind of charge was specifically dealt with under another provision of the Criminal Code, namely, section 319(2) — the anti-hate law. The complaint against Zundel, Justice McLachlin stated, "presents the Court with the question of whether a much broader and vague class of speech — false statements ... likely to injure ... public interest — violates the Charter of Rights and Freedoms."

In no small measure, the extent to which both the Charter guarantee of freedom of expression and its potential limit applied to the false news law depended on the public policy and its importance embodied in that law. Put somewhat differently, if the false news law reflected an important public policy, then the Court would have to ask: Can that policy be allowed while at the same time protecting the Charter guarantee of freedom of expression? If, on the other hand, there was little if any public policy behind the false news law, then the Court could give fuller sweep to freedom of expression.

Justice McLachlin, speaking for the Court majority, found that the false news law lacked any purpose, and that its terms were too vague to enforce. She said that the law had been placed in the Criminal Code almost by what appeared to be an accident. Initially, when the law was enacted by the British Parliament in 1275, it was intended to curb political criticism in the form of writing and songs against the "Great Lords" of the day, though its terms applied to all. (Songsters — called minstrels — tended to be the media of the day for the peasants who made up the greater part of the population.) It also was used to limit blood feuds between members of the nobility, who might otherwise have taken revenge for what they deemed personal insults. But, even then, the law was seldom used.

Justice McLachlin said she could find no evidence as to why the false news law was kept in Canada after it had been ended in England. Aside from the present case against Zundel, the law had been used in Canada only three times between 1892 and 1992.

Perhaps, even more to the point, *there were* basic *difficulties in enforcing the law*. On the whole, unless parties otherwise agree, juries determine questions of fact. And, Justice McLachlin asked, how were juries to determine the kind of facts at issue in the Zundel case? These were among the questions juries were to consider:

- How is the truth of a historic fact to be proved? How does one prove what actually occurred in the past?
- The fact questioned must be false. In addition, however, the individual accused must subjectively believe the fact in question is false. How is that subjective belief to be proved?
- What is the public interest that is likely to be injured as a result of the public airing of false facts?

THE CHARTER APPLIED

Justice McLachlin, in a forty-three-page opinion, ruled that *the false news law conflicted with the Charter guarantee of freedom of expression* which, she said, "serves to protect the right of the minority to express its view, however unpopular it may be.... The view of the majority has no need of constitutional protection; it is tolerated in any event.... A law which forbids expression of a minority or false view on pain of criminal prosecution and imprisonment, on its face offends the purpose of the guarantee of free expression.... It is often the unpopular statement which is most in need of protection under the guarantee of free speech."

The right of free expression, Justice McLachlin stated, will promote truth and political or social participation, furthering self-fulfillment in society. Toward that end, she continued, the Court should not be concerned with the content of a message.

Still, the question remained: Could the false news law be saved or permitted to stand, even though it violated the fundamental freedom of free expression under section 2(b) of the Charter? Section 1 of the Charter allows for this to happen if the violation reflects "reasonable limits prescribed by law as can be demonstrably justified in a free and democratic society."

It is here that Justice McLachlin again reviewed the purpose (or lack of one) of the false news law. Section 1 of the Charter placed the burden on the Crown to prove an overriding public objective to justify setting aside the Charter guarantee of freedom of expression. In this regard, Justice McLachlin made it clear that such an objective is to be found by what Parliament meant when it enacted the false news law — *not by what judges might find in reading other purposes into the law at a later point in time.* She wrote:

Can it be said in these circumstances that the Crown has discharged the burden upon it of establishing that the objective of the [false news law] is ... substantial ... [and] of sufficient importance to justify overriding the constitutional guarantee of expression? I think not.

It may be that section 181 [the false news law] is capable of serving legitimate purposes. But no objective of ... substantial concern has been identified in support of it being kept in our Criminal Code. Other provisions, such as section 319(2) of the Criminal Code, deal with hate propaganda more fairly and more effectively. Still other provisions seem to deal adequately with matters of ... state security.

THE DISSENT

Justices Peter Cory and Iacobucci, joined by Justice Charles Gonthier, issued an eighty-six-page dissent which centred on the facts at trial related to the distribution of hate propaganda by a group of neo-Nazis, sometimes disguised as "revisionist" historians. The dissent recognized that section 2(b) of the Charter had been violated — but only minimally. After all, *the false news law condemned false assertions of fact, not opinion that the speaker knew to be false.*

These are elements that the dissent would have required by way of proving a fact to be false:

- The statement must be definite to convey meaning.

- The statement must be one which can be proved objectively.
- The statement must be in a setting where it is clear that facts are represented.

The dissent would have saved the false news law through section 1 of the Charter as a reasonable limit on freedom of expression imposed in a free and democratic society. The dissent stated:

> The deceptive nature of the deliberate publication of false statements of fact may, in certain circumstances, be even more [wrongful] than the publication of hateful opinions which at least express the beliefs of the publisher.
>
> Thus, section 181 [the false news law] fulfills an important role in a multicultural and democratic society. It emphasizes the repugnance of Canadian society for the wilful publication of known falsehoods that cause injury through their attacks upon groups identifiable under ... the Charter and therefore on society as a whole.

PUBLIC OR PRIVATE PROSECUTION?

Question: As noted, Citron brought a private prosecution against Zundel under the false news law. Why wasn't a prosecution brought under the anti-hate law which, according to the majority opinion in the Zundel case, might have been more relevant? After all, the anti-hate law is an indictable offence punishable by up to two years imprisonment on conviction.

Answer: There is no right to a private prosecution under the anti-hate law. Only the Crown can lay charges. And, apparently, the attorney general at the time was not convinced that such an action would succeed.

ERNST ZUNDEL: BACKGROUND

Ernst Zundel, a German citizen, came to Canada in 1958 at the age of nineteen. He settled initially in Montreal. His status was that of landed immigrant. As the years went by, he twice sought citizenship, but his application was rejected each time.

THE INFLUENCE OF CANADA'S "FUHRER"

In Montreal, Zundel came under the influence of Adrien Arcand, self-styled "Fuhrer" of Canada, who in 1934 established the Parti national social chrétien that had as its emblem a swastika surrounded by maple leaves, with a Canadian beaver at the crown. The party was stridently anti-communist, separatist, and anti-Semitic. It sought the resettlement of Canadian Jews near Hudson Bay.

At the start of the Second World War, Arcand claimed that he and his then-new party, the National Unity Party, would take over Canada. Instead, he was interned by the federal government in New Brunswick for the duration of the war, and his party was declared illegal. He returned to Quebec after the war, in 1945, and continued his Nazi preaching. He died in 1967 (*The Canadian Encyclopedia,* Year 2000 Edition).

Arcand was reportedly "extraordinarily well-read, artistically gifted and highly knowledgeable in Western philosophy." His "intellectual approach" appealed to Zundel. Further, Zundel became convinced that postwar Germany had been represented on the world stage by spineless persons bent on ongoing apology for their wartime sins — sins which he denied, including denial that the Holocaust had actually occurred.

Like Arcand, Zundel entered politics. He even ran for the Liberal Party leadership in 1968 against Pierre Trudeau. Zundel got publicity, but he was no challenge to Trudeau.

ZUNDEL: SELF-STYLED "GURU OF THE RIGHT"
Zundel moved to Toronto where he became a highly successful graphic artist. That skill, coupled with his insistence that the Holocaust had never happened, led him to establish a publishing organization, Samisdat Publishers.

With Zundel as its head, presenting himself as "the guru of the right ... the teller of uncomfortable truths," the publishing house — and his presence — became a world focal point for so-called historic revisionist propaganda. But, it wasn't just printed matter that was the medium of Zundel's message. As well, there was a slick website. His message went where it was intended: Europe and the United States.

The German government reacted. In Zundel's absence (*in absentia*), a prosecution was carried out and Zundel was convicted of the crime of Holocaust denial.

Zundel was quoted as saying: "If I may quote the much-maligned Adolf Hitler: 'If you discover a true personality, treat it with kid gloves because nature makes so few personalities.' With all modesty, I would have to say that, like Charles de Gaulle [World War II French leader and later President of France], *l'état, c'est moi*" (*Globe and Mail,* March 2, 2005).

In 1985 (spurred on by Sabina Citron, the individual who launched a private prosecution under the false news law, later joined by the Crown), Zundel was tried and convicted twice for spreading false news likely to cause social unrest, more particularly, Holocaust denial. (See "You Be the Judge: The Case of 'False News,'" above.) On each of the more than forty days of trial, Zundel arrived at his hearing with a uniformed group of young followers in hard hats labelled: *Freedom of speech.*

After his conviction, there were deportation hearings initiated by the Canadian government. Zundel arrived at these hearings carrying a large crucifix. He acknowledged later that it was a stunt for publicity — a stunt that succeeded. He intended to project the profile of a long-suffering martyr, and to have news of his status carried worldwide.

After the Supreme Court reversed the false news conviction in 1992, Zundel was spared deportation. In 2000 he moved to Pigeon Forge, Tennessee, apparently hoping to obtain U.S. citizenship. There, he and his wife operated a website that spread the same message he had delivered in Canada.

U.S. authorities acted to deport him for immigration violations. He was deported to Canada in May 2003. There, Canadian officials, using the legislative power of the *security certificate* established by Parliament in response to the bombings in the U.S. on September 11, 2001, arrested Zundel.

The Canadian claim was that Zundel was a threat to national security. Canadian officials sought to deport him to Germany. Zundel, assisted by counsel, resisted the deportation effort. Pending the hearings (which took place over forty-three days), and with appeals in the interim, Zundel was held in solitary confinement. The end result was an order, not then appealed, that resulted in his deportation on March 2, 2005, to Germany, where he was arrested, denied bail, and held on charges of Holocaust denial.

HATE AND NATIONAL SECURITY: THE ZUNDEL STORY CONTINUED

Ernst Zundel was deported from the United States to Canada. This action was taken because Zundel, not a U.S. citizen, was found to have violated U.S. immigration laws. His status in Canada was that of a landed or permanent resident. But, he was not a Canadian citizen.

THE NATIONAL SECURITY CERTIFICATE: PROCEDURE

On April 30, 2003, two months after Zundel's return to Canada, two federal ministers (the minister of citizenship and immigration and the solicitor general of Canada) signed a national security certificate that denied him entry to Canada on grounds of national security. Their legal authority came from the *Immigration and Refugee Protection Act, Statutes of Canada 2001*, chapter 27 (IRPA).

Zundel was placed in a detention centre in Toronto pending hearings and decision under the IRPA. However, while we will describe those hearings and the final decision, this point is noted: Zundel could have ended his detention at any time by agreeing to return to Germany where he was a citizen. He refused to do this. He wanted to remain in Canada, and thus was compelled to challenge the security certificate under a law enacted soon after the September 11, 2001, terrorist bombings in the U.S.

The IRPA sets out the grounds for a certificate to issue:

§34(1) A permanent resident or a foreign national is inadmissible on security grounds for
    (a) engaging in an act of espionage or an act of subversion against a democratic government, institution or process as they are understood in Canada;

(b) engaging in or instigating the subversion by force of any government;

(c) engaging in terrorism;

(d) being a danger to the security of Canada;

(e) engaging in acts of violence that would or might endanger the lives or safety of persons in Canada; or

(f) being a member of an organization that there are reasonable grounds to believe [is engaging in terrorism].

On the day the certificate was issued and Zundel was arrested, Justice Pierre Blais of the Federal Court of Canada was assigned to review and hear matters relating to the certificate. On May 1, the next day, he held a teleconference hearing in private (that is, with Crown counsel but without Zundel or his counsel) to determine whether there was a *reasonable basis for the certificate to be issued and for Zundel to be detained*. (The IRPA requires that such a hearing be held within seven days of it being issued and that the hearing be held in private. Further, the law requires regular review by a judge until a final decision is made.)

Justice Blais determined that there was a reasonable basis for the issuance of the certificate, and he ordered a hearing to determine whether Zundel should be deported. That hearing was one in which Zundel and his counsel had the right to appear, present evidence, and be given a summary of evidence taken in secret — up to the point that the judge believed disclosure of information or the identity of witnesses would not endanger national security.

Zundel was jailed (even placed in solitary confinement) for almost two years, then forcibly removed from Canada. The hearings that resulted were not conducted as regular criminal proceedings in two ways:

1. As noted, where national security was found by the judge to be involved (a decision made, as described, in private), the evidence and the identity of the witnesses were kept

confidential. Zundel and his counsel were entitled to a summary of evidence within the bounds of national security, again as determined by the judge. But they were entitled to nothing more. The general rule in criminal proceedings, and reflected in the Charter, is that the accused has the right to know, confront, and cross-examine his/her accusers. *But, this is a general rule and the same Charter allows for exception where that limitation is described by law and is seen as necessary in a free and democratic society.*

2. The criminal law ordinarily requires that the Crown prove its case beyond a reasonable doubt. A national security certificate will be sustained *if there are reasonable grounds for doing so.* What does this mean? In effect, this means that the ministers who signed the certificate had a good faith belief that the charges set out were true, based on believable evidence. Justice Blais stated: "To demonstrate that the certificate is reasonable, the Ministers must only demonstrate that there is a serious possibility, based on credible evidence, that Mr. Zundel is inadmissible on one of the grounds of inadmissibility provided by section 34 of the IRPA [quoted above]. In fact, the Ministers do not have to conclusively demonstrate any of the allegations of inadmissibility."

The national security certificate involving Zundel stated that he was detained, and it sought his deportation on the ground that he was a threat to the security of Canada.

FINDINGS OF THE FEDERAL COURT
Counsel for Zundel argued that his client had committed no acts of violence. Nor had he been convicted of any crimes under valid laws. Justice Blais said that the points were not relevant to the *validity of the certificate.* He wrote:

I would point out that there is no requirement that an individual who is inadmissible to Canada on security grounds be personally involved in acts of violence. Such an interpretation is short-sighted and not in keeping with the ruling of the Supreme Court of Canada in *Suresh v. Canada (Minister of Citizenship and Immigration)*, [2002] 1 *Supreme Court of Canada Reports* 3, that danger to the security be given a "fair, large and liberal interpretation." There is therefore no requirement that criminality be determined in order for a permanent resident or a foreign national to be found to be a danger to the security of Canada.... Rather, ... the threat that a person may constitute a danger to the security of Canada must be substantial and based on an objectively reasonable suspicion.

THE DETAILED EVIDENCE

The findings of Justice Blais cover more than sixty-five pages. It is enough to say here that he emphasized that, on more than one occasion, the court noted that the hearing was not a criminal proceeding. Under the law, the task of Justice Blais was to determine whether there was a reasonable basis for supporting the national security certificate. His task was not to determine whether the high standard of proof in a criminal case had been sustained.

Justice Blais said that there was more than enough evidence to support the security certificate. Key to his findings was the connection between Zundel and White Supremacists who, among other things, were bent on destabilizing the German government. We quote here a portion of Justice Blais's findings that spoke of the importance of Zundel in the White Supremacist movement and of Zundel's associations with those who support that movement:

[According to] the Security Intelligence Report of which Mr. Zundel was provided a summary, White Supremacists are defined as racists, neo-Nazis and anti-Semites who use violence to achieve their political objectives. Leading White Supremacists may inspire others to use or threaten use of violence.

Mr. Zundel is viewed by White Supremacists as a leader of international significance and was viewed as the patriarch of the Movement in Canada for decades. Mr. Zundel is one of the world's most prominent distributors of revisionist neo-Nazi propaganda through the use of facsimiles, courier, telephone, mail, media, shortwave radio transmissions, satellite videos and the Internet, through his web site the Zundelsite, which is a platform for financing and contains White Supremacist documents as well as hyperlinks to other White Supremacist web sites. The Security Intelligence Report concludes that based on the evidence that has been provided, Mr. Zundel is playing a critical role in the Movement, both in Canada and internationally.

Documents issued by Mr. Zundel over the years show his intention to destabilize the legal and legitimate democratic government of Germany. The evidence also demonstrates a clear determination to disseminate copious amounts of documentation and information from Canada to Germany, using Canadian soil to advance his goal of undermining the German government.

Furthermore, the Ministers have provided public and *in camera* [secret] evidence that Mr. Zundel has extensive involvement with contacts within the violent, racist, right wing movement. These contacts encompass individuals and organizations in Canada and abroad.

Mr. Zundel has always supported the ideology of the White Supremacist Movement, one which is based on the fundamental belief that the white race is an endangered species in need of protection as a result of non-whites and Jews seeking to attack the foundation of western civilization. Blacks in particular are seen as intellectually inferior, while Jews are viewed as conspiring to gain control of the world through manipulation of financial markets, the spread of communism, pornography and general moral degeneracy. The government is viewed with suspicion as it is seen to be controlled by a Jewish conspiracy referred to as Zionist Occupation Government (ZOG). These fundamental beliefs lead to anti-Semitic, racist, anti-immigration, anti-democratic, anti-human rights and anti-homosexual attitudes.

The Nazi Party under Adolf Hitler in Germany in the 1930s and 1940s is notoriously well known; what is less known is the Canadian version which was developed over the 1940s and the 1950s under Adrien Arcand, who promoted Hitler as a saviour of Christianity and formed the Parti national social chrétien in the 1930s. That party then merged with the Canadian Nationalist Party from the West to form the National Unity Party. Later, in the 1960s, the Canadian Nazi Party became the National Socialist Party and Mr. Zundel explained how he was influenced by Mr. Arcand himself whom he met when he arrived in Canada in the 1950s.

At the conclusion of World War II, the enthusiasm of those Nazi parties around the world was greatly reduced; nevertheless, there still remained some desire to support this neo-Nazi approach. Mr. Zundel is among the few people that worked hard to maintain that support and who went to great lengths to try and establish some credibility to the neo-Nazi movement. He also tried by all means possible to develop and maintain a global network of all groups that have an interest in the same right wing extremist neo-Nazi mind-set.

The Ministers filed as evidence a document by the Security Intelligence Review Committee (SIRC), entitled *The Heritage Front Affair Report*. The Ministers zeroed in on a particular part of this report and I quote: "Finally, we would like to put on the record our unshakeable conviction that the Government of Canada, through all means at its disposal, should continue to ensure that it is always aware of what is going on within extreme right wing racist and neo-Nazi groups. Canadians should never again repeat the mistakes of the past by underestimating the potential for harm embodied in hate-driven organizations." [Section 13.12 of the SIRC document.]

The analysis of the public documents provided by the Ministers, and the evidence that was heard over the 43 days of public hearings in this case, depict a man who publicly has always tried to demonstrate his opposition to violence.

Nevertheless, for more than 20 years, Mr. Zundel continuously maintained close relationships with individuals around the world who are clearly identified as members of the White Supremacist Movement. Mr. Zundel admitted in his own testimony that through different means of communication, he is in touch with people in 42 countries.

Mr. Zundel maintained a close association with Wolfgang Droege and even admitted that he believed Mr. Droege was involved in terrorist activities in the United States, including attempting to invade the small Republic of Dominica to establish a White Supremacist government. Mr. Zundel's house on Carlton Street in Toronto was akin to a revolving door for Mr. Droege, as well as every other member of the White Supremacist Movement in Canada or from abroad. These members were always welcome at his house, which had transformed from a residence, into a command centre for people and organizations worldwide involved in the White Supremacist Movement.

Furthermore, Wolfgang Droege and Marc Lemire, two successive presidents of the Heritage Front, spent a lot of time in Mr. Zundel's house. Mr. Lemire, the last known president of the Heritage Front, was working for Mr. Zundel part-time, and then full-time for many years until Mr. Zundel left for the United States.

Mr. Zundel also maintained a close association with Terry Long and the Aryan Nations. Mr. Long was a very zealous activist in Canada, and was depicted as one of the most extreme of the leaders of the Aryan Nations, an organization founded by Richard Butler in 1974 that has among its goals, the elimination of Jews and all minorities, as well as the creation of a White homeland in the North Western United States.

CLAIMS OF NON-VIOLENCE AND FREEDOM OF EXPRESSION

Justice Blais addressed Zundel's claims of non-violence and freedom of expression. He wrote:

> It is troubling to hear Mr. Zundel proclaim that he is defending freedom of expression and advocating the use of non-violence while, at the same time, spending most of his time working in close quarters with the most extreme individuals and organizations in the White Supremacist Movement.
>
> If, as Mr. Zundel claims, he is not on side with extremists, is not on side with people claiming that the Jews should be eliminated, and is not on side with Canadian members of the Heritage Front that wanted to create a list of members of the Jewish Movement for future retaliation, then how can he agree to participate in a meeting of the Heritage Front as a guest speaker, surrounded and supported by members of extremist White Supremacist groups in Canada?
>
> If, as Mr. Zundel said, the Heritage Front, a group described as the most powerful racist gang to hit Canada since the real Nazis back in the Dirty Thirties, was not a good idea, then why would he hire the president of that organization, Mr. Lemire, as a part-time and then full-time employee in his own personal residence?
>
> If, as Mr. Zundel stated, Mr. Droege is a terrorist and was totally ill-advised with everything he has done, be it in the United States or as leader of the Heritage Front, then how can he allow him to enter his house on a daily basis?

If, as Mr. Zundel claims, it is not a good idea to use web sites to disseminate messages of racial hatred and incite violence in the pursuit of White Supremacist objectives and that it is not a good idea to post on the Internet a practical guide to Aryan revolution which included chapters on assassinations, terror bombings, sabotage and racial wars, then why would he qualify Bernard Klatt, the man responsible for posting this guide, as a gentle person, and maintain contact with Mr. Klatt over the years?

If, as Mr. Zundel believes, Tom Metzger is a violent person involved in criminal activities and in promoting a campaign of hatred which led to the beating death of an Ethiopian immigrant by two skinheads in the United States, for which Mr. Metzger had to subsequently pay a $12.5 million judgment after being found responsible by a civil court of that beating, and if he disagrees with the kind of racist cartoons made by and promoted by Mr. Metzger, and if he thinks that the White Aryan Resistance Hate Page web site, which depicted grotesque and disgusting pictures of Negro and Jewish cartoons is not a good idea, then why does he cooperate with Mr. Metzger, Mr. Butler and the Aryan Nations?

If, as Mr. Zundel was well aware, Bela Ewald Althans was convicted, among other things, of incitement to hatred under German law, and imprisoned after being found guilty of denying the Holocaust and insulting the state and the memory of the dead, and if Mr. Zundel knew that the presiding judge has called Mr. Althans "a moral arsonist" who is not a violent man but is still just as dangerous to the community, then why did he keep Mr. Althans as his personal representative in Europe and in Canada to disseminate his publications and organize tours for him in Europe?

If, as Mr. Zundel acknowledged, Dennis Mahon and the Oklahoma Excalibur were involved in extremist comments, even advocating revolution and a violent overthrow of the Canadian government in a meeting in Canada in 1992, then why did he agree to assist Mr. Mahon in designing a cover page for his publication?

These serious contradictions required explanation; if Mr. Zundel did not subscribe to the views expressed by all those people and organizations, then he should have clearly expressed, both publicly and privately, his total opposition to the kind of material, propaganda, violence and hatred promoted by those individuals and associations. I simply cannot accept the proposition that Mr. Zundel is a pacifist while, at the same time, he continues to maintain a close association and to support the above-mentioned extremists.

Mr. Zundel has himself admitted that he has a large ego. He tried to diminish the importance of his admission that he was somehow a "guru of the right." Nevertheless, he is proud of the influence he has on all the people and organizations that are mentioned in the Summary. He always tries to distance himself from the violence and extremist views proliferated by those people and organizations, but he does not want to sever these ties; he wants to maintain his influence on them. He did not want to be seen as a leader of the Heritage Front, he even mentioned that he was not a member of that organization. But the leaders of this organization were spending most of their time in his house to hear his suggestions and to follow his advice. I remember how proud he was when he mentioned in cross-examination that his Zundelsite received hits from 400,000 people a month, and that after his arrest, the number grew to 1.2 million people accessing his web site every month; his tone and body language were more telling than anything of the proudness he had, realizing that after decades, more than a million people every month were in touch with his writings.

Faced with the evidence that was provided by the Ministers, I have no hesitation in concluding that pursuant to section 33 and to paragraph 34(1)(d) of the IRPA, there are reasonable grounds to believe that Mr. Zundel is inadmissible on security grounds for being a danger to the security of Canada.

Mr. Zundel has associated with, supported and directed members of the Movement who in one fashion or another have sought to propagate violent messages of hate and have advocated the destruction of governments and multicultural societies. Mr. Zundel's activities are not only a threat to Canada's national security but also a threat to the international community of nations. Mr. Zundel can channel the energy of members of the White Supremacist Movement from around the world, providing funding to them, bringing them together and providing them advice and direction.

It would be illusory to believe that the White Supremacist Movement is receding. While it is true that the detention of Mr. Zundel may have taken the wind out of the sails of his followers, the White Supremacist network is still very much alive and active. The use of the Internet has created new methods of communication which have replaced traditional ones. No longer must halls or pubs be rented in order to have meetings; rather, communication can now take place easily and anonymously between adherents of the White Supremacist Movement, as well as anyone else curious enough to visit web sites or log onto chat rooms dedicated to keeping this network alive.

The physical presence of Mr. Zundel is not necessary to maintain the sustenance [support] of this network. Nonetheless, Mr. Zundel's freedom, following two years of incarceration, would no doubt galvanize the White Supremacist Movement. Mr. Zundel has the funding, the support, an established infrastructure, a means of communication to the masses via his Zundelsite as well as numerous individuals who are prepared to do his bidding. Mr. Zundel is capable of bringing all this back together and once again spurring the White Supremacist Movement.

In this case, I have no doubt regarding the fairness and legality of the process and I have no doubt that the evidence in support of the certificate conclusively established that Mr. Zundel represents a danger for the security of Canada and that the certificate signed by the Minister of Citizenship and Immigration and the Solicitor General of Canada is reasonable.

NO APPEAL

Within hours of Justice Blais's decision, the federal government moved to deport Zundel. He received a letter which stated in part: "The purpose of this letter is to inform you that your removal to Germany is imminent.... Please note that you are entitled to a total of two suitcases with a maximum weight of 32 kilograms each."

Zundel determined not to seek any appeal from the decision of Justice Blais. His claim that if returned to Germany he might well be subject to torture by German authorities had been reviewed and rejected by Justice Blais (*Globe and Mail,* February 26, 2005).

CHALLENGE QUESTION

A COURT'S POWER – THE MINISTERS' CHOICE

Q: Suppose that a court orders the disclosure of evidence coming from a national security certificate which the signing ministers still believe should be kept secret. And, suppose that reviewing courts support the trial court's order. What, if any, choice do the ministers have regarding such disclosure?

Justice Blais took up this question. He said that the ministers always have the right to withdraw the evidence initially presented in private. This means that the court cannot look to such evidence in coming to its decision. Justice Blais also noted that such a decision might affect other parts of the case necessary for a final decision. He wrote:

> The decision [for production of infor-
> mation relating to the national security

certificate] is made by the judge and not by the Ministers. If the judge arrives at the conclusion that part of the evidence should be disclosed and the Ministers still believe that its disclosure would [hurt] national security, the Ministers may withdraw the evidence that is proposed. Sometimes, this is a difficult task because the disclosure of one part of the evidence could divulge information that would make possible the identification of the sources which not only would be injurious to national security but also to the security of persons. This problem is described as the mosaic effect....

This means for instance that evidence, which of itself might not be of any particular use in actually identifying the threat, might nevertheless require [it] to be protected if the mere divulging of the fact that CSIS [Canadian Security Intelligence Service] is in possession of it would alert the targeted organization to the fact that it is in fact subject to electronic surveillance or to a wiretap or to a leak from some human source within the organization.

ZUNDEL DEPORTED AND CHARGED IN GERMANY: HOLOCAUST DENIAL, ITSELF, A CRIME

On March 1, 2005, before dawn, Ernst Zundel was placed on a flight from Toronto to Germany. Canadian authorities had deported him. At an earlier time, faced with the possibility of deportation to Germany, Zundel was quoted as saying: "[Being deported to Germany] would be like being sentenced to paradise.... I can't be punished by being sent to a place where there are comforts, money and supporters."

However, on arrival in Germany, Zundel was charged with the offence of denial of the Holocaust — a specific crime in Germany. He was taken before a judge, informed of his rights, and jailed pending trial, bail having been denied.

The Bundesgerichtshof, Germany's highest federal court, set out the reasoning for making Holocaust denial, itself, a crime — with no exception for claimed freedom of opinion:

> The historical fact that human beings were separated in accordance with the descent criteria of the so-called Nuremberg laws and were robbed of their individuality with the objective of their extermination, gives to the Jews living in the Federal Republic [of Germany] a special personal relationship to their fellow citizens; in this relationship, the past is still present today.
>
> It is part of their personal self-image that they are seen as attached to a group of persons marked out by their fate, against which group there exists a special moral responsibility on the part of everyone else and which is a part of their dignity. Respect for this personal self-image is for each of them really one of the guarantees against a repetition of such discrimination and a basic condition for their life in

the Federal Republic. Whoever seeks to deny those events denies to each of them individually this personal worth to which they have a claim. For those affected, this means the continuation of discrimination against the group of human beings to which he belongs, and with it against his own person.

GERMAN LAW APPLIED

The Bundesgerichtshof has given the law against Holocaust denial a wide application, one that caught Zundel. In December 2000, it ruled that the law can be imposed against foreigners who upload content on the Internet that is illegal in Germany. This means, for example, that content from websites outside Germany are subject to legal challenge.

That ruling emanates from a case involving Frederick Toben, a Holocaust revisionist (like Zundel) who was arrested for distributing leaflets in Germany that claimed that the Holocaust had never happened. German courts sentenced Toben to ten months in prison for distributing the leaflets, and for making available on his website Holocaust denial material.

Toben appealed the latter element of his conviction, stating that his website is based in Australia and therefore is not subject to German law. Though German-born, Toben has lived in Australia for most of his life and is a citizen of that country. The Bundesgerichtshof has upheld the conviction.

The German decision bears some similarity to a French case. Recently, France's high court issued several rulings barring Yahoo, the global Internet portal, from auctioning Nazi memorabilia in France.

REASON FOR DIFFERENCE: A GERMAN POLICE RESPONSE

Hans-Gertz Lange, a spokesperson for the Verfassungsschutz (the German counterpart to CSIS and the RCMP) said: "The best chance to fight against right-wing material on the Internet is on an international level. But when I think of the U.S. or Canada, it's extremely unlikely that they'll change their laws in accordance with ours. Their concept of freedom of speech is tied up with their history; our laws against incitement to racial hatred are tied up in ours."

THE SENTENCING OF ZUNDEL
On February 15, 2007, the German court imposed on Ernst Zundel the maximum sentence allowed under German law: five years imprisonment with a release date of 2010. The German court ruled that the two years Zundel spent imprisoned in Canada under a security certificate could not be taken from the five-year sentence. However, the two years he had been confined in Germany were taken into account. The Zundel conviction and sentence was upheld on appeal.

The trial itself had lasted for the better part of two years. This was due, in part, to Zundel's counsel and their trial tactics. He retained counsel initially not authorized to practise law in Germany, and he later included a counsel who shouted racial anti-Semitic slurs in the court and was carried from the room (and was later subject to discipline). In final arguments, Zundel's counsel read passages from Adolf Hitler's *Mein Kampf* — the then young German dictator's views on racial purity.

ANOTHER POINT OF VIEW ON THE DEPORTATION OF ZUNDEL
The following is an extract from an editorial that appeared in the *Globe and Mail* on February 26, 2005. It argues that the rule of law was diminished and that respect for civil liberties was sacrificed through the use of the security certificate to hold, to take secret testimony from, and then to deport Zundel:

The mightiest weapon of the state was used against [Zundel], and denied him bail, because he associates with unsavoury people, holds hateful views, and is a hero to racists around the world. To realize how foreign that is to the purpose for which the certificate was created, consider the grounds available in the Immigration and Refugee Protection Act for justifying the certificate's use: that the person has engaged in terrorism or subversion; belongs to a group that one might reasonably believe has engaged or will engage in acts of violence that might endanger the lives or safety of persons in Canada. Mr. Zundel could not be held under any of those grounds. Instead, Judge Blais upheld his certificate on the ground that "he is a danger to the security of Canada."

The case is unpersuasive. Mr. Zundel designed the cover of a magazine for a reprehensible white-supremacist publication in Oklahoma "to improve the quality of the media presentation. Nevertheless, he did nothing to improve or to change the quality of the content." Mr. Zundel had extremists in his house, and employed the last-known president of the racist Heritage Front. He "maintained a close association" with; he "stayed in touch" with; he maintained "close contacts" with. Guilt by association? Judge Blais himself acknowledges the weakness that runs through his argument. "Mr. Zundel, *even if he is not supportive of their more radical and demonstrative ideas,* recognizes the efforts of organizations such as the Aryan Nations and the White Aryan Resistance" [italics: *Globe and Mail*].

The closest thing to a smoking gun is that Ernest Zundel's activities are illegal in Germany and Austria, which make it a jailable offence to deny the Holocaust. That might have been reason for Germany to try to extradite Mr. Zundel, who is a German citizen; it did not justify the use of a Canadian security certificate. However hateful Ernst Zundel may be — and he is hateful, no question — abusing the authority to issue security certificates does more than hurt Mr. Zundel. It diminishes the rule of law, and sacrifices respect for civil liberties on the altar of expedience (*Globe and Mail,* February 26, 2005).

STILL ANOTHER POINT OF VIEW

This letter to the editor appeared in the *Globe and Mail* on March 10, 2005. It was written by Joel Richler, Chair, Canadian Jewish Congress, Ontario Region, Toronto.

Imagine you learn that an individual living on Canadian soil has spent the better part of twenty years creating linkages between himself and white supremacists in Canada and internationally.

Imagine that this individual takes egotistical pride in styling himself as a "guru of the right."

Imagine that this individual describes his own role in the right-wing movement as being where he "sows the seeds and other people then build on those ideas."

Imagine that the movement to which this individual claims the status of "guru" is one that holds the fundamental belief that the white race is an endangered species in need of protection as a result of non-whites and Jews attacking the foundation of Western civilization.

Imagine that this individual styles himself as a pacifist — a statement that a Federal Court judge viewed as hypocritical because the individual maintained close association over the years with groups and individuals who hold violent views.

Imagine that this individual is able to argue his case before the Federal Court for 43 days over a period of almost two years, and still claims he has been denied justice.

Imagine that this individual, after due process and in accordance with the laws of Canada, is removed from the country to stand trial on criminal charges in another democratic country.

Can you imagine yourself having any doubts regarding the rightful deportation of Ernst Zundel?

PRIVATE SCHOOL PRANK SUPPRESSED

Two elite Toronto private schools were in an uproar over an anti-Semitic website that lasted only six days, but resulted in the expulsion of three boys and the suspension of four more.

On April 22, 2005, a grade ten student at Royal St. George's College went home and set up a Microsoft chat board. The site — accessible only to his fellow classmates at Royal St. George's (a boys' school) and grade ten students at Branksome Hall (a girls' school), as well as a third private school — invited subscriptions. Within days, nearly one hundred signed up.

The board quickly took on a life of its own, and another Royal St. George's student started cyber rooms on the site, such as "Gas Chamber" and "The Reichstag." Several classmates posted photographs of Nazi rallies and Jews being tortured in a concentration camp.

Four girls from Branksome — using the pseudonym "Rod" — sent a message to the chat board asking that the material be removed. The response? A Royal St. George's student attacked the critics, using homophobic, anti-Semitic language that witnesses termed "horrifying." The girls informed their principal and their parents. Branksome's principal contacted the headmaster of Royal St. George's at noon on April 27. By 4:00 p.m., the chat board was down.(*Globe and Mail*, May 3, 2005; *Toronto Star*, May 3, 2005; *Toronto Star*, May, 2005; *Globe and Mail*, May 7, 2005).

THE TORONTO STAR RESPONDS

On May 4, 2005, the following editorial titled "Standing Up to Hatred" appeared in the *Toronto Star*:

> Ignorance, intolerance and hate are not limited to any social or economic group. Sadly, they are traits seen in both rich and poor, young and old, uneducated and highly schooled.
>
> That became clear when it was revealed that a student at Royal St. George's College, a private boys' school in Toronto, recently posted Nazi-themed images on an Internet chat room set up by a classmate.
>
> When several students at Branksome Hall, a nearby private girls' school, asked that the content be removed, two other Royal St. George's students responded with a stream of vicious anti-Semitic invective that a Branksome Hall official called "graphic, vile and truly shocking."
>
> Of course, some might argue, kids will be kids. That sometimes means acting impulsively and foolishly.

But that does not mean the students who posted the images and messages should be let off lightly for their abhorrent expressions of hate.

While the students, one of whom is Jewish, apparently did not commit the odious acts on school property, the schools have dealt with the incident swiftly and appropriately.

Royal St. George's has expelled the boy who posted the photos and the two boys who responded to the complaints. Both schools have also held assemblies to educate students about anti-Semitism. That sends the message to all students at these schools that anti-Semitism will not be tolerated. It is the right message.

The incident also reminds us that Canadians must remain vigilant against expressions of hate.

B'nai Brith Canada reports anti-Semitism is on the rise here. The group recorded 857 incidents last year, a 47% jump over 2003 and the highest number in the 22 years since it started keeping track.

This disturbing figure shows intolerance and hate are alive and well.

What can be done?

Tolerance must be nurtured both at home and at school. Children must learn the troubling histories of the Holocaust, the slave trade, the internment of Japanese Canadians during World War II and other human rights atrocities.

Most important, we all must be ready to stand up to bigotry and racism, wherever it confronts us (*Toronto Star,* May 4, 2005).

DIFFERENCES: U.S.A./CANADA

The Constitution of the United States with its Bill of Rights, including the right of free speech, often is compared with the Canadian Charter of Rights and Freedoms. There are, however, important differences, not only in the constitutional texts but also in how those texts are applied.

For example, the U.S. free speech right, reading the text alone, contains no qualifier such as that found in section 1 of the Charter. Yet, the interpretation of that text is another matter. Consider the U.S. Supreme Court decision in *R.A.V. v. City of St. Paul, Minnesota,* 60 *United States Law Week* 4667 (June 22, 1992). There, all nine justices of the U.S. Supreme Court struck a city ordinance (law) directed at expressions of hate against others because, for example, of their race.

The *expression* was the burning of a cross on the front lawn of the newly-purchased residential home of Russ and Laura Jones and their five children — an African-American family. The cross was ignited around midnight on a summer night. Mrs. Jones later said: "If you are black and you see a cross burning, you know it's a threat, and you imagine all the church bombings and lynchings that have gone on before, not so long ago…. A burning cross is a way of saying: *We're going to get you.*"

Investigators identified those responsible as six young men: a seventeen-year-old high school dropout; the eighteen-year-old son of a neighbour of the Jones family; and four juveniles. Before the burning, investigators said the six had been drinking and talking about causing some "skinhead trouble" and "burning some niggers."

THE LAW AND DECISION
One of those charged challenged the constitutionality of the city ordinance used to convict, which stated: "Whoever places on public or private property a symbol, object, appellation [name], characterization or graffiti, including but not limited to a burning cross or Nazi swastika, which one knows or has reasonable grounds to

know arouses anger, alarm or resentment in others on the basis of race, color, creed, religion or gender, commits disorderly conduct and shall be guilty of a misdemeanor."

The case eventually came before the Supreme Court of the United States. All nine justices agreed that the city ordinance was unconstitutional, and it was declared invalid. However, the justices wrote four different opinions. We will focus of the opinion of Justice Antonin Scalia who spoke for himself and four other justices, thus constituting the majority.

The city ordinance was declared unconstitutional for what it didn't include. Justice Scalia stated:

> Those who wish to use fighting words in connection with other ideas — to express hostility, for example, on the basis of political affiliation, union membership, or homosexuality — are not covered. The First Amendment [of the Constitution, dealing with freedom of speech] does not permit the City of St. Paul to impose special prohibition on those speakers who express views on disfavored subjects…. The point of the First Amendment is that majority preferences must be expressed in some manner other than silencing speech on the basis of content….
>
> The question in this case, therefore, is whether content discrimination is reasonably necessary to achieve St. Paul's compelling interests; it plainly is not. An ordinance not limited to the favored topics, for example, would have achieved precisely the same effect….
>
> In fact, the only interest distinctively served by the content limitation is that of displaying the city council's special hostility toward the particular biases thus singled out. That is precisely what the First Amendment forbids. The politicians of

St. Paul are entitled to express that hostility — but not through the means of imposing unique limitations upon speakers who … disagree.

REFERENCES AND FURTHER READING

Alphonso, Caroline, and Joe Friesen. "Jewish Pupil Among Three Expelled." *Globe and Mail,* May 3, 2005.

Black, Debra. "Racist Incident Offers Lessons." *Toronto Star,* May 3, 2005.

Fraser, Angus. 1992. *The Gypsies.* Cambridge, MA: Harvard University Press.

Globe and Mail. "The Zundel Certificate." February 26, 2005.

Hancock, Ian. 1987. *The Pariah Syndrome: An Account of Gypsy Slavery and Persecution.* Ann Arbor, MI: University of Michigan Press.

Makin, Kirk. "Supreme Court Orders New Trial for Skinheads." *Globe and Mail,* February 24, 2005.

_____. "Court Finds Zundel Can Be Deported." *Globe and Mail,* February 25, 2005.

_____. "Zundel Won't Fight Deportation Order." *Globe and Mail,* February 26, 2005.

_____. "Holocaust Denier is Returned." *Globe and Mail,* March 2, 2005.

Moore, Oliver. "Anti-Semitic Incidents Soar." *Globe and Mail,* March 16, 2005.

Small, Peter. "Six Protestors Face New Trial Over Hatred Charges." *Toronto Star,* February 25, 2005.

Teotonio, Isabel. 2005. "Anti-Semitism on Website has Elite Schools in Uproar." *Toronto Star,* May 2.

Toronto Star. "Standing Up to Hatred." May 4, 2005.

Wong, Jan. "15 Minutes of Shame." *Globe and Mail,* May 7, 2005.

3

CHAPTER 3

TEACHING HATRED: DANGEROUS LESSONS

We begin this chapter with a single case, *Ross v. New Brunswick School District No 15*, [1996] 1 *Supreme Court of Canada Reports* 825 (the Ross case). The central issues go to tensions between freedom of expression, mixed in part with claims of religious freedom and the statutory duty imposed on public school boards to deliver non-discriminatory education. (More will be said of religious freedom in Chapter 4.)

For twenty years, Malcolm Ross had been a public school teacher in New Brunswick. In the community, he was known to have anti-Semitic beliefs that reflected his strongly held religious ideology. In 1977 he had publicly stated: "Christian civilization is being undermined and destroyed by an international Jewish conspiracy." Over the years he had publicly repeated his anti-Jewish beliefs in published pamphlets, letters to the editor, and public television appearances. However, he did not repeat these beliefs in his classrooms.

In 1988 a complaint was filed with the New Brunswick Human Rights Commission, which had broad statutory authority to prevent and remedy discrimination in providing public services (such as education) for a range of reasons including "race, colour, religion, national origin [and] ancestry." The complaint cited what it claimed were anti-Semitic acts on the part of Ross dating more than a decade earlier.

The complaint stated that the school board, Ross's employer, had a statutory responsibility to provide for the delivery of non-discriminatory educational services. This, said the complaint, was not done. Ross's out-of-school statements, in effect, "poisoned" the educational environment.

The New Brunswick Human Rights Act gave broad authority to tribunals it established to hear complaints (called boards of inquiry) to make findings of fact and develop appropriate remedies should human rights violations be found. The legislature gave broad powers to such tribunals. Their findings of facts were to be accepted so long as, on the record, there was a reasonable basis for doing so. Put another way, a reviewing court was not to substitute its findings merely because it might have come to a different factual conclusion.

What should be the remedy on a finding of violation of a human rights code? Was a court to yield to the judgment of an administrative board? What is a court's role, and especially that of the Supreme Court of Canada, when the effect of an administrative decision is to stifle freedom of expression guaranteed by section 2(b) of the Charter?

Among the questions raised in this chapter are:

- Are there limits to the personal opinions teachers can express in a classroom?
- Outside the classroom, does a teacher have the right of freedom of expression?
- What role do human rights laws have in filtering what teachers can say?

FINDINGS AND ORDER IN THE ROSS CASE

Eight years after the New Brunswick Board of Inquiry had been established and its findings and order entered, the matter came before the Supreme Court of Canada for review. The decision of the Supreme Court was unanimous. It was handed down by Justice La Forest, a native of New Brunswick. This is the Court's view of the facts in the Ross case, as stated by Justice La Forest:

> The factual context within which these issues arise is as follows. On April 21, 1988, [David] Attis [a parent of children who were students at the school where Ross taught] filed a complaint with the Human Rights Commission of New Brunswick, alleging that the Board of School Trustees, District No. 15, violated §5 of the Human Rights Act by discriminating against him and his children in the provision of accommodation, services or facilities on the basis of religion and ancestry. [Attis] alleged that the School Board, by failing to take appropriate action against the respondent Ross, a teacher working for the School Board who publicly made racist, discriminatory and bigoted statements, condoned [justified] his anti-Jewish views and breached §5 of the Act by discriminating against Jewish and other minority students within the educational system served by the School Board.
>
> On September 1, 1988, a human rights board of inquiry was established to investigate the complaint. In the complaint, Attis, a Moncton resident, described himself as a Jew. He alleged that the discriminatory conduct by the School Board occurred from March 29, 1977 to April 21, 1988, and arose out of the actions of Ross, a teacher at Magnetic Hill School. The latter made racist and discriminatory statements in published writings and in appearances on public television. In his published writings, which consist of four books or pamphlets published from 1978 to 1989, and

three letters to New Brunswick newspapers, Ross ... argued that Christian civilization was being undermined and destroyed by an international Jewish conspiracy. [The hearings before the Board of Inquiry lasted for twenty-one days.]

At the time of the hearing before the Board of Inquiry, Ross did not have a homeroom class, but was a modified resource teacher. He had been employed at the school since September 1976, and before that as a teacher at the Birchmount School. Concerns about the respondent's writings had been expressed publicly since 1978, when the Chairman of the Human Rights Commission had sent a letter to the School Board requesting that his classroom performance be supervised. *By 1987, the School Board's response to the controversy had become a public issue and the Department of Education of New Brunswick became involved* [emphasis added].

In 1988 the School Board instituted disciplinary action against Ross. On March 16, 1988, he was reprimanded and warned that continued public discussion of his views could lead to further disciplinary action, including dismissal. He was also informed that the warning was applicable to his out-of-school activities. The reprimand remained in force until September 20, 1989. On November 21, 1989, Ross made a television appearance [where his allegations of Jewish "conspiracy" were again vetted] and was again reprimanded by the School Board on November 30, 1989.

The Board of Inquiry found there was no evidence of any direct classroom activity by Ross on which to base a complaint under §5 of the

Human Rights Act. However, it also found that his off-duty comments denigrated the faith and belief of Jews. It concluded that his actions violated §5(1) of the Act and that there was no reasonable excuse to justify the discriminatory effect of those actions. It further found that the School Board was liable for any breaches of §5 of the Act by its teachers and, as such, the School Board was also in breach of §5 of the Act. The Board concluded that the School Board discriminated by failing to discipline Ross meaningfully in that, by its almost indifferent response to the complaints and by continuing his employment, it endorsed his out-of-school activities and writings. This, it held, resulted in an atmosphere where anti-Jewish sentiments flourished and where Jewish students were subject to a "poisoned environment" within the School District "which has greatly interfered with the educational services provided" to Attis and his children.

EXAMINATION OF EVIDENCE BY THE COURT

In seeking whether there was reasonable proof to support the Board of Inquiry's findings, the Supreme Court examined the evidence. It was not enough that Ross made what appeared to be anti-Semitic comments and that he expressed them publicly. The central question was whether those comments either actually, or on the face of it, could be seen as reasonably likely to infect the educational environment. And this, in turn, led the Court to ask about the nature and the role of public schools.

Again, Justice La Forest, speaking for all nine justices, said the evidence supported a finding that Ross's comments could have had the effect of infecting the school environment. And, in making this finding, Justice La Forest commented on the public nature and, in a sense, the public policy role of education. He wrote:

> Ross does not contest the [Board of Inquiry's] findings in relation to his off-duty conduct and publications, or in relation to anti-Semitic incidents in the School District. His point is that there is no direct evidence linking these two findings. I am unable to agree with this contention. For the following reasons, I am of the view that the finding of discrimination against the School Board must stand.
>
> The Board of Inquiry heard evidence of the nature of Ross' writings, publications and statements, which include a letter to the editor of *The Miramichi Leader*, a local television program interview, and the four books or pamphlets listed in the order. The Board found, without hesitation, that these publications contain *prima facie* [on the face of it] discriminatory comments against persons of Jewish faith and ancestry. Their effect, in its view, was to denigrate the faith and beliefs of Jews and to incite in Christians contempt for those of the Jewish faith by their assertion that they seek to undermine freedom, democracy and Christian beliefs and values. The Board further found that Ross' comments speak of Jews as the synagogue of Satan, and accuse Judaism of teaching that "Jesus Christ is a bastard, a lewd deceiver, a false prophet who is burning in Hell" and that the Virgin Mary is a whore. Ross was also found to have continuously alleged that the Christian faith and way of life are under attack as a result of an international conspiracy headed by Jews. The Board characterized his primary purpose as being "to attack

the truthfulness, integrity, dignity and motives of Jewish persons." It also made a finding of fact as to Ross' notoriety in the community of Moncton, and that continued media coverage of his statements and writings over an extended period contributed to his views having gained notoriety in the community and beyond. *Given that these findings are findings of fact supported by the evidence, they are entitled to deference by this Court upon review, in light of the relative expertise of the Board in relation to the art of fact-finding in a human rights context, and I accept them* [emphasis added].

On the basis of the factual evidence disclosing the substance of Ross' off-duty conduct, and the notoriety of this conduct in the community and beyond, the Board considered how such conduct impacted upon Ross' teaching ability. In concluding that conduct of the type evinced by the facts of this case may undermine the capacity of a teacher to fulfil his or her position, the Board [of Inquiry] noted: "In the case of the teacher who has proclaimed the discriminatory views publicly, the effect may adversely impact on the school community. It may raise fears and concerns of potential misconduct by the teacher in the classroom and, more importantly, it may be seen as a signal that others view these prejudicial views as acceptable. It may lead to a loss of dignity and self-esteem by those in the school community belonging to the minority group against whom the teacher is prejudiced."

The [Nova Scotia Human Rights] Act does not prohibit a person from thinking or holding prejudicial views. *The Act, however, may affect the right of that person to be a teacher when those views are publicly expressed in a manner that impacts on the school community or if those views influence the treatment of students in the classroom by the teacher* [emphasis added].

Justice La Forest then looked to the evidence presented to the Board of Inquiry as to Ross's outside conduct as it impacted on the school environment:

> The Board heard evidence from two students in the School Board, whom it found to be credible witnesses. The students described in detail the educational community in the school district. They gave evidence of repeated and continual harassment in the form of derogatory name calling of Jewish students, carving of swastikas by other students into their own arms and into the desks of Jewish children, drawing of swastikas on blackboards, and general intimidation of Jewish students.
>
> [The Complainant's daughter,] Yona Attis, one of the student witnesses, gave evidence of one occasion on which she had planned to attend [Ross's] school to watch a gymnastic competition, when she was advised [by a teacher] that she could not go to the school because that was "where the teacher who hates Jews works." The teacher referred to was identified as [Ross]. Yona Attis stated that she attended the competition, but that she felt scared while there, and anxious "that someone was going to come up behind [her] and grab [her] and beat [her] up or something." Further evidence of taunting and intimidation of the Jewish students was disclosed in her testimony, including incidents of shouting and signalling of the "Heil, Hitler" salute.

What this evidence discloses is a poisoned educational environment in which Jewish children perceive the potential for misconduct and are likely to feel isolated and suffer a loss of self-esteem on the basis of their Judaism.

It is to be noted that the testimony of the students did not establish any direct evidence of an impact upon the school district caused by [Ross'] off-duty conduct. Notwithstanding this lack of direct evidence, the Board concluded: *"Although there was no evidence that any of the students making anti-Jewish remarks were directly influenced by any of Malcolm Ross' teachings, given the high degree of publicity surrounding Malcolm Ross' publications it would be reasonable to anticipate that his writings were a factor influencing some discriminatory conduct by the students"* [emphasis added].

WEIGHING THE EVIDENCE: THE "SPECIAL" ROLE OF TEACHERS

Justice La Forest then weighed the evidence set out by the Board of Inquiry. Speaking for a unanimous Supreme Court, he set out the standard of "reasonableness" both as to the findings of fact and the inferences to be drawn from those findings. Those inferences had to be drawn in the context of the nature of public schools, bearing in mind the role they are to perform in society. He stated:

This inference drawn on the basis of what is reasonable to anticipate must be considered in light of whether, in the circumstances, it is reasonable to anticipate that [Ross'] off-duty conduct "poisoned" the educational environment in the School Board and whether it is sufficient to find discrimination according to a standard of what is reasonable to anticipate as the effect of the off-duty conduct. I will consider each of these points in turn.

A school is a communication centre for a whole range of values and aspirations of a society. In large part, it defines the values that transcend society through the educational medium. The school is an arena for the exchange of ideas and must, therefore, be premised upon principles of tolerance and impartiality so that all persons within the school environment feel equally free to participate. As the Board of Inquiry stated, a school board has a duty to maintain a positive school environment for all persons served by it.

Teachers are inextricably linked to the integrity of the school system. Teachers occupy positions of trust and confidence, and exert considerable influence over their students as a result of their positions. The conduct of a teacher bears directly upon the community's perception of the ability of the teacher to fulfil such a position of trust and influence, and upon the community's confidence in the public school system as a whole. Allison Reyes considers the importance of teachers in the education process and the impact that they bear upon the system, in "Freedom of Expression and Public School Teachers" (1995), 4 *Dalhousie Journal of Legal Studies* 35. She states, at p. 42: "Teachers are a significant part of the unofficial curriculum because of their status as 'medium.' In a very significant way the transmission of 'prescribed messages' (values, beliefs, knowledge) depends on the fitness of the 'medium' (the teacher)."

By their conduct, teachers as "medium" must be perceived to uphold the values, beliefs and knowledge sought to be transmitted by the school system. The conduct of a teacher is evaluated on the basis of his or her position, rather than whether the conduct occurs within the classroom or beyond. Teachers are seen by the community to be the medium for the educational message and because of the community position they occupy, they are not able to "choose which hat they will wear on what occasion" (see *Re Cromer and British Columbia Teachers' Federation* (1986), 29 *Dominion Law Reports (4th series)* 641 (British Columbia Court of Appeal), at p. 660); teachers do not necessarily check their teaching hats at the school yard gate and may be perceived to be wearing their teaching hats even off-duty. Reyes affirms this point in her article, *supra*, at p. 37: "The integrity of the education system also depends to a great extent upon the perceived integrity of teachers. It is to this extent that expression outside the classroom becomes relevant. *While the activities of teachers outside the classroom do not seem to impact directly on their ability to teach, they may conflict with the values which the education system perpetuates*" [emphasis in original].

Then, Justice La Forest cited and quoted from a British Columbia court of appeal decision that dealt with ongoing responsibilities of off-duty teachers to their school board employer. He stated:

I find the following passage from the British Columbia Court of Appeal's decision in *Abbotsford*

*School District 34 Board of School Trustees v.
Shewan* (1987), 21 *British Columbia Law Reports
(2d series)* 93, at p. 97, equally relevant in this
regard: "The reason why off-the-job conduct may
amount to misconduct is that a teacher holds a
position of trust, confidence and responsibility. If
he or she acts in an improper way, on or off the
job, there may be a loss of public confidence in
the teacher and in the public school system, a loss
of respect by students for the teacher involved,
and other teachers generally, and there may be
controversy within the school and within the
community which disrupts the proper carrying
on of the educational system."

It is on the basis of the position of trust and
influence that we hold the teacher to high standards both on and off duty, and it is an erosion
of these standards that may lead to a loss in the
community of confidence in the public school
system. I do not wish to be understood as advocating an approach that subjects the entire lives
of teachers to inordinate scrutiny on the basis of
more onerous moral standards of behaviour. This
could lead to a substantial invasion of the privacy
rights and fundamental freedoms of teachers.

*However, where a poisoned environment
within the school system is traceable to the off-duty
conduct of a teacher that is likely to produce a cor-
responding loss of confidence in the teacher and the
system as a whole, then the off-duty conduct of the
teacher is relevant* [emphasis added].

EVIDENCE AGAINST ROSS

The nature of Ross's position as a public school teacher allowed the Board of Inquiry to review the facts to determine whether his off-duty activities reflected anti-Semitism that could be imputed to his employer, the school board, in the sense of infecting the learning environment of the schools it administered. Justice La Forest, for the Supreme Court, citing an earlier decision handed down by then Chief Justice Brian Dickson, restated the test for finding a teacher outside employment improper: "Could or would [it] give rise to public concern, unease and distrust of [the teacher's] ability to perform [his/her] employment duties?"

Justice La Forest reviewed the findings of the Board of Inquiry and accepted them. In doing so, he agreed that *the school board had a positive responsibility to prevent such action by Ross as might "poison" the school educational environment*. It was a duty, he said, the school board did not carry out:

> The Board found that [Ross's] off-duty comments impaired his ability to fulfil his teaching position. The teaching occupation is uniquely important. This, combined with the substance of [Ross's] writings and statements and the highly public media through which they were disseminated, i.e. television and published works, supports the conclusion that this finding of the Board is correct....
>
> In the present case, I note that the Board was presented with evidence ... on the likely effects of [Ross's] conduct. [It was] stated that the Jewish students having a general knowledge of [Ross] could be fearful of him. Indeed, this is borne out in Yona Attis' testimony, and is supported by the pervasive awareness of [Ross's] conduct throughout the community. [There was] evidence that it

was possible that Jewish students would be nega-
tively influenced by [Ross] and that they would see
themselves as the subject of suspicion, distrust and
isolation. [Such evidence was that] there might be a
reluctance on the part of Jewish parents to become
involved in the school system that might deter
other Jewish families from moving to Moncton.

[After] a television interview given by [Ross]
in 1989, the School Board itself characterized the
effect produced by [Ross's] conduct: "The climate
created by this aggressive approach creates hostility that permeates and interferes with the desired
tolerance required by the school system to show
respect for the rights of all students and their families to practise their religious faith."

I conclude ... that a reasonable inference is
sufficient in this case to support a finding that
the continued employment of [Ross] impaired
the educational environment generally in creating a poisoned environment characterized by a
lack of equality and tolerance. [Ross's] off-duty
conduct impaired his ability to be impartial and
impacted upon the educational environment in
which he taught.

The Board found that School District No. 15
discriminated contrary to §5 of the Act. It found
the School Board had been reluctant to take disciplinary action against [Ross], [despite] the publicity his conduct received and the awareness on
the part of the School Board of the situation in
the community at large. In effect, its passivity sig-
nalled a silent condonation [acceptance] of, and
support for [Ross's] views. The Board found an
obligation within the school community "to work

towards the creation of an environment in which students of all backgrounds will feel welcomed and equal" (p. 83). It stated (at p. 80): "In such situations it is not sufficient for a school board to take a passive role. A school board has a duty to maintain a positive school environment for all persons served by it and it must be ever vigilant of anything that might interfere with this duty."

I am in complete agreement with this statement, and I refer to the findings of the Board that the School Board failed to maintain a positive environment. The School Board, it found, was reluctant to become involved and was slow to respond when complaints about [Ross] were first raised.

The evidence discloses that as early as 1978, letters were sent to the Director of School District No. 15 regarding concerns about [Ross's] continued employment, and requesting his dismissal. The position of the School Board at that time was expressed by Nancy Humphrey, Chairperson of the School Board, as being that [Ross] could do what he wanted on his own time. From 1979 through 1984, [Ross's] in-class teaching was monitored; however, in 1983, media coverage of the respondent's activities was augmented.

By 1986–87, the School Board was receiving approximately 10 to 20 letters a week concerning [Ross]. After he wrote an article in *The Miramichi Leader* in 1986, a scheme directed at more frequent monitoring of his class was put into place. By 1987, the public controversy surrounding [Ross] had grown concerning the level of the School Board's involvement, and the question as to whether [Ross] would be charged under the hate literature provisions of the Criminal Code was raised. A committee was established by the School Board in 1987 to review the possible impact of the issue on the learning environment. This committee, however, was found by the Board of Inquiry to have failed to address the questions it should have and to appreciate the subtle forms discrimination may take.

According to the acting superintendent, Cheryl Reid, in 1988 [Ross] was "cautioned strongly against any further publications regarding [his] views." In the same year, the first disciplinary action was taken against [Ross], at which time he was informed that any further publications, or public discussions of his views or works, would result in greater disciplinary action and possible dismissal. A reprimand in the form of a "gag order" was placed on his personal file. Subsequent to this, three complaints were filed against him. The Human Rights Commission began an investigation in response to these complaints. The Board of Inquiry, however, found that the School Board strongly resisted the investigation. The investigation recommended that the Board of Inquiry be established in 1988.

In March 1989, the School Board adopted Policy No. 5006, intended to ensure that students were offered a positive and safe learning environment, in which they were taught respect for the rights and freedoms of the individual. In September 1989, the School Board decided to remove the "gag order" from [Ross's] file. Two months later, [Ross] appeared on television to express and discuss his views. The School Board responded by ordering a severe reprimand to [Ross], by way of letter, requesting that he refrain from "publicly assailing" another religion. The Board of Inquiry found it difficult to understand why the School Board only gave [Ross] a reprimand at this time as opposed to terminating his employment, given that [Ross] had been sent a strongly worded letter along with a copy of Policy No. 5006 making the intention of the new policy very clear to him.

A review of this chronology led the Board of Inquiry to conclude that the School Board had discriminated in its failure to take a proactive approach to the controversy surrounding [Ross], the effect of which was to suggest the acceptance of [Ross's] views and of a discriminatory learning environment. The finding of discrimination against the School Board is supported by the evidence and I accordingly see no error in this finding of the Board of Inquiry.

RELEASING THE ROSS DECISION — A SYMBOLIC GESTURE?

The Supreme Court released the Ross decision on Wednesday, the eve of the Passover — an important Jewish holiday marking the freedom of the Jews from Egyptian bondage and their movement toward receipt of the Ten Commandments. Ordinarily, Supreme Court decisions are released on Thursdays. The *Globe and Mail* suggested that this was a symbolic gesture on the part of the Court (*Globe and Mail,* April 4, 1996).

YOU BE THE JUDGE

ROSS: THE ORDER AND FREEDOM OF EXPRESSION

The case that follows is a continuation of the Ross case. Recall that the Supreme Court of Canada affirmed the finding of the New Brunswick Human Rights Board of Inquiry: There had been discrimination in violation of the provincial human rights act in the failure of the public board of education to take proactive action against a public school teacher who publicly and widely spread anti-Semitic attacks.

Now, however, the question went to the kind of order imposed on Ross. In this regard, remember that the function of a reviewing court, including the Supreme Court of Canada, was to ask whether the order entered by the Board of Inquiry was reasonable in the light of the evidence, and whether it was valid in law.

THE FACTS

The following was the order entered by the Board of Inquiry:

(2) That the School Board:
   (a) immediately place Malcolm Ross on a leave of absence without pay for a period of eighteen months;
   (b) appoint Malcolm Ross to a non-teaching position if, within the period of time that Malcolm Ross is on leave of

absence without pay, a non-teaching position becomes available in School District 15 for which Malcolm Ross is qualified. The position shall be offered to him on terms and at a salary consistent with the position. At such time as Malcolm Ross accepts employment in a non-teaching position, his leave of absence without pay shall end.

(c) terminate Malcolm Ross' employment at the end of the eighteen month leave of absence without pay if, in the interim, he has not been offered and accepted a non-teaching position.

(d) terminate Malcolm Ross' employment with the School Board immediately if, at any time during the eighteen month leave of absence or if at any time during his employment in a non-teaching position, he:

(i) publishes or writes for the purpose of publication, anything that mentions a Jewish or Zionist conspiracy, or attacks followers of the Jewish religion, or

(ii) publishes, sells or distributes any of the following publications, directly or indirectly:

- *Web of Deceit*
- *The Real Holocaust (The Attack on Unborn Children and Life Itself)*
- *Spectre of Power*

• *Christianity vs. Judeo-Christianity*
(The Battle for Truth)

THE ISSUES

- Did the order respond to the facts as found by the Board of Inquiry?
- Was the order valid under the Charter?

POINTS TO CONSIDER

- The purpose of any order under the New Brunswick Human Rights Act is to remedy the wrongs found. Such orders are not intended to punish.
- Ross has a sincere belief, based on religious convictions, in his anti-Semitic claims.
- It is clear that the order of the Board of Inquiry does violate the freedom of expression guaranteed under section 2(b) of the Charter. Compliance with the order of the Board of Inquiry would deny Ross the right to express his anti-Semitic views.
- It is possible for the Board order to be sustained if it meets the tests put under section 1 of the Charter, which provides that government may set *reasonable limits prescribed by law as can be demonstrably justified in a free and democratic society.*
- However, such "limits" must be the minimum necessary to achieve the reasonable government goals.

- The Board found, and the Supreme Court accepted, that an important and pressing government goal, as expressed in provincial legislation, among other objectives is to provide New Brunswick students with a public education that is tolerant and fosters a democratic society.

DISCUSSION

In the Ross case, Justice La Forest had no difficulty in finding that the Board of Inquiry order did indeed violate Ross' rights to freedom of religion and expression as guaranteed by sections 2(a) and (b) of the Charter. In doing so, he accepted that Ross' views reflected sincerely held religious beliefs.

Justice La Forest quoted from an earlier Supreme Court of Canada decision in *The Queen v. Big M Drug Mart Ltd.,* [1985] 1 *Supreme Court of Canada Reports* 295, where then Justice Dickson stated: "A truly free society is one which can accommodate a wide variety of beliefs, diversity of tastes and pursuits, customs and codes of conduct.... The essence of the concept of freedom of religion is the right to entertain such religious beliefs as a person chooses, the right to declare religious beliefs openly and without fear of hindrance or reprisal, and the right to [demonstrate] religious belief by worship and practice or by teaching and [making those views known to others]."

But, these rights could and were limited by the province's human rights act. These limitations fit within the meaning of section 1 of the Charter. The human rights act was a reasonable limit prescribed by law and it was demonstrably justified in a free and democratic society. Indeed, the human rights act was intended, among other things, to hold others with tolerance and respect — not to defame them because of their religion.

This is, in part, what Justice La Forest stated — again, on behalf of a unanimous Supreme Court. It is important to note that the Court drew a line between that which was necessary to curb Ross's behaviour as a teacher and what he might otherwise do as an employee of the school district in a non-teaching role. In a non-teaching role, Justice La Forest made it clear that Ross was free to speak so far as asserting his Charter rights in that regard were concerned:

> The Board's order asserts a commitment to the eradication of discrimination in the provision of educational services to the public. Based upon the jurisprudence, Canada's international obligations, and the values constitutionally entrenched, the objective of the [Board's] order is clearly pressing and substantial....
>
> The [Human Rights] Act in question is conciliatory in nature and makes no provision for criminal sanctions. It is, therefore, well suited to encourage reform of invidious [malicious] discrimination. The Board focused on providing relief in crafting its order, and sought, as much as possible, to avoid punitive effects.
>
> The Board made a finding that §5(1) of the [Human Rights] Act "guarantees individuals freedom from discrimination in educational services available to

the public." In order to ensure a discrimination-free educational environment, the school environment must be one where all are treated equally and all are encouraged to fully participate. Teachers must ensure that their conduct transmits this message of equality to the community at large, and are expected to maintain these high standards both in and out of the classroom.

ROSS REMOVED AS TEACHER
Justice La Forest continued:

The Board held that the fact that [Ross] publicly made anti-Semitic statements contributed to the "poisoned environment" in the school system, and that it was reasonable to anticipate that his statements and writings had influenced the anti-Semitic sentiment in the schools.... In this case, I think it is sufficient that the Board found it "reasonable to anticipate" that there was a causal relationship between [Ross's] conduct and the harm — the poisoned educational environment.

In my view, this finding must depend upon [Ross's] maintaining a teaching position. The reason that it is possible to "reasonably anticipate" the causal relationship in this appeal is because of the significant influence teachers exert on their students and the stature associated with the role of a teacher. *It is thus necessary to remove [Ross] from his teaching position to ensure that no influence of this kind is exerted by him upon his students and to ensure that the educational services are discrimination-free. The order seeks to remove [Ross] from his teaching position through clauses 2(a), (b) and (c). These clauses are rationally connected to the objective of the order* [emphasis added].

LIMITS TO THE BOARD'S ORDER

Justice La Forest said, however, that there were limits to the Board's order. Recall that the Board could only impose the minimum limits on Ross required to deal with his anti-Semitic activity affecting students.

If Ross were granted employment in a non-teaching capacity in the school system, removed from contact with students as such, Justice La Forest set boundaries to the restraints that the Board might impose on Ross. He stated:

> My concerns lie with clause 2(d) of the order, which I reproduce below:
> "(2) That the School Board:
> (d) terminate Malcolm Ross' employment with the School Board immediately if, at any time during the eighteen month leave of absence or if at any time during his employment in a non-teaching position, he:

(i) publishes or writes for the purpose of publication, anything that mentions a Jewish or Zionist conspiracy, or attacks followers of the Jewish religion, or

(ii) publishes, sells or distributes any of the following publications, directly or indirectly:

- *Web of Deceit*
- *The Real Holocaust (The Attack on Unborn Children and Life Itself)*
- *Spectre of Power*
- *Christianity vs. Judeo-Christianity (The Battle for Truth)*"

I will deal with that part of the order under "minimal impairment." An impairment must be minimal to the extent that it impairs the right no more than is necessary....

The tailoring process seldom admits of perfection and the courts must accord some leeway to the legislator. If the law falls within a range of reasonable alternatives, the courts will not find it overbroad merely because they can conceive of an alternative which might better tailor objective to infringement....

In arriving at its order, the Board considered the alternatives available to remedy the discrimination. It concluded that the removal [of Ross] from the classroom was "the only viable solution." In the course of examining alternative solutions, the Board found that the situation could not be corrected through an apology and renunciation of his views by [Ross]. Nor could it be corrected through continual monitoring of [Ross's] classroom, as the Board considered the influence of a teacher to be "so much more complex than the formal content of any subject matter taught by the teacher." The Board also rejected the exclusion of Jewish children from [Ross's] class or school, emphasizing the importance of accessibility to schools within a public school system. Finally, it concluded that the situation could not be dealt with through monetary compensation to Attis for pain and suffering.

In making its order, the Board stated: "This Board of Inquiry has carefully reviewed the writings and statements of Malcolm Ross and his reaction to directions from the School Board to refrain from such writings and publications. Malcolm Ross' commitment to his beliefs and intent to publicly proclaim these beliefs through his writings, even following clear direction from the School Board, is obvious."

The order, in clauses 2(a), (b) and (c), was carefully tailored to accomplish its specific objective, i.e. to remedy the discriminatory situation in School District 15 created through the writings and publications of Malcolm Ross. Any punitive effect is merely incidental. In my view, clauses 2(a), (b) and (c) minimally impair the respondent's freedom of expression and freedom of religion. In relation to clause 2(d), however, I arrive at a different conclusion.

THE BOARD ORDER APPLIED TO A NON-TEACHING POSITION
Justice La Forest stated:

> The Board found that "Section 5 [of the New Brunswick Human Rights Act] strives for a discrimination-free environment in the school system so that everyone within School District 15 can enjoy the public educational services provided by the School Board without discrimination. Malcolm Ross, by his writings and his continued attacks, has impaired his ability as a teacher and cannot be allowed to remain in that position if a discrimination-free environment is to exist."
>
> The Board, on the basis of the evidence before it, found that [Ross] had to be moved out of his teaching position. By occupying a position of great influence, his presence contributed to a discriminatory educational environment. The Board did not find that [Ross's] presence in a non-teaching

position would compromise the ability of the School Board to create a discrimination-free environment. Indeed, their order made provision for the possibility that the respondent would occupy a non-teaching position.

It may be that the continued presence of [Ross] in the School Board produces a residual poisoned effect, even after he is removed from a teaching position, and it may be that this is what clause 2(d) seeks to address. Given [Ross's] high profile and long teaching career, I acknowledge that the problem in the School District could remain for some time.

However, the evidence does not support the conclusion that the residual poisoned effect would last indefinitely once Ross has been placed in a non-teaching role. For that reason, clause 2(d) which imposes a permanent ban does not minimally impair the respondent's constitutional freedoms. Clause 2(d) is not justified under section 1 [of the Charter].

The deleterious [harmful] effects of clauses 2(a), (b) and (c) of the order upon [Ross's] freedom of expression and freedom of religion are limited to the extent necessary to the attainment of their purpose. [Ross] is free to exercise his fundamental freedoms in a manner unrestricted by this order, upon leaving his teaching position. These clauses only restrict [Ross's] freedoms to the extent that they prohibit [Ross] from teaching, based upon the exercise of his freedom of expression and freedom of religion. [Ross] is not prevented from holding a position within the School Board if a non-teaching position becomes available; furthermore, he is to be offered a non-teaching position if it becomes available on terms and at a salary consistent with the position. In my view, the objectives of preventing and remedying the discrimination in the provision of educational services to the public outweigh any negative effects on the respondent produced by these clauses.

THE ROSS CASE — AN APPEAL BEYOND THE SUPREME COURT

Ross appealed the unanimous decision of the Supreme Court of Canada to the United Nations Human Rights Committee. He argued that, as a result of the 1996 decision of the Supreme Court of Canada, he had been denied his right to freely express his religious opinions when he was transferred to a non-teaching position. (The school district was later reorganized, and Ross was laid off.)

Removal from his teaching position, Ross said, violated his freedom of thought, conscience, and religion, and his freedom of expression as guaranteed by Articles 18 and 19 of the International Covenant on Civil and Political Rights. Canada had agreed to abide by that Covenant's "Optional Protocol" which allows individuals who have exhausted all their national (called "domestic") remedies to file complaints with the UN's Human Rights Committee.

The UN committee panel consisted of fifteen members. They unanimously rejected Ross's claim on December 12, 2000.

The committee members found that the limit to Ross's *freedom of religion* was permitted because it was prescribed by law and necessary to protect the fundamental rights and freedoms of others.

In a similar vein, all but one of the committee members found that the limit to Ross's *freedom of expression* was allowed since it was provided by law and necessary to respect the rights and reputations of others.

The other committee member was even more emphatic. That member concluded that Ross's freedom of expression had not been restricted because freedom of expression necessarily involved duties and responsibilities. Article 20 of the International Covenant prohibits advocacy of religious hatred that constitutes incitement to discrimination, hostility, and violence.

"We believe that justice was done," New Brunswick Human Rights Commission chair Dr. Patrick Malcolmson said. "This decision shows that the balance that our laws strike between freedom of expression and freedom from discrimination is consistent with international human rights standards."

Professor Tom Kuttner, who was a counsel *pro bono* [without compensation and in the public interest] for the commission, said: "The decision is an important affirmation by the international community of the integrity of the Canadian human rights regime in general, and that of New Brunswick in particular, and, for this, we can all be justly proud."

CHALLENGE QUESTION

ANOTHER POINT OF VIEW

The *Globe and Mail* editorially disagreed with the decision of the Supreme Court of Canada in the Ross case. It set out what it considered the relevant portions of the decision of Justice La Forest, and then it offered the following critique:

> We do not share the view that the legal, constitutionally protected activities of teachers on their own time should qualify as grounds for dismissal. The role model basis for assessing teacher competence once disqualified divorced people from teaching in most provinces. Many other grounds could be asserted for similar punitive action on the basis of a person's identity outside the school. In our view, teachers have a right to personal lives equal to that of any other group.
>
> We do not agree that an employer shows support for the off-work views of any employee by the simple fact of employing that person. Failure to take a positive approach to a controversy more probably reflects the employer's respect for the employee's private rights.
>
> The Supreme Court asserts that no direct evidence of harm to students is required to justify the dismissal of a teacher on role-model grounds.... We find the

standard of proof here to be unacceptably low. The Court itself is the authority which states that high school students are greatly affected by the simple stature of their teachers. The Court then sets the very low hurdle of reasonable anticipation of harm to justify Mr. Ross' dismissal on those same grounds.

This case ties imputed and flaccid standards of judgment to speculative standards of proof to justify the firing of a teacher who is exercising his otherwise legal and constitutional rights (albeit most offensively). We dissent (*Globe and Mail*, April 5, 1996).

Q. Has the editorial considered all the relevant factors reviewed by the Supreme Court in the Ross decision?

The editorial apparently did not consider *hate directed against an identifiable group*. The editorial seemed to have accepted that what Ross said and had published was entitled to the *same level of protection as every other form of expression*. This was not the view of the Court in its unanimous ruling.

The Charter itself draws a line of difference between freedoms that are protected, such as freedom of expression and freedom of religion (section 2), and limits that may be placed on those freedoms (section 1).

The Court made it clear that Ross's freedom of expression and freedom of religion were violated by the order of the Board of Inquiry. The question before the Court, at that point, was whether the limits placed on Ross's freedoms were justified under section 1 of the Charter.

It was in the context of section 1 that the Court drew a line of difference between expression of hate and the core values intended to be protected under section 2 in terms of freedom of expression. The core values referred to, said the Court, citing precedent, are those that include "the search for political, artistic and scientific truth, the protection of individual autonomy and self-development, and the promotion of public participation in the democratic process."

Referring to an earlier decision, Justice La Forest quoted from the opinion of then Chief Justice Dickson:

> I am very reluctant to attach anything but the highest importance to expression relevant to political matters. But given the unparalleled vigour with which hate propaganda repudiates and undermines democratic values, and in particular its condemnation of the view that all citizens need to be treated with equal respect and dignity so as to make participation in the political process meaningful, I am unable to see the protection of such expression as integral to the democratic ideal so central to the section 2 [freedom of expression] rationale.

This meant, said Justice La Forest, that limits placed on expressions of hate should attract a "less searching degree of scrutiny and be easier to justify under section 1 [of the Charter]." In this regard, it was the Board of Inquiry which held the human rights hearings and found the facts that pointed to a "poisoned" educational environment that could reasonably be anticipated to be linked to Ross's off-duty activities. It was a review of those findings in the context of the expressions of hatred that allowed the Court to approve that portion of the Board of Inquiry ending Ross's teaching career in the public school system of the province.

ROSS, FREE EXPRESSION, AND THE CARTOON BATTLE

Josh Beutel was a well-known freelance political cartoonist for the *Saint John Telegraph-Journal* and the *Evening Times-Globe* (Saint John, New Brunswick newspapers). During the course of the litigation involving Malcolm Ross, Beutel had drawn and published a number of cartoons relevant to the conflict.

Following the Supreme Court's decision in the Ross case, Beutel was asked and agreed to speak before a meeting of the New Brunswick Teachers' Association. He spoke about Ross and, in the process, showed a number of cartoons concerning the issues raised. Ross responded by bringing a suit for defamation. Specifically, Ross claimed that Beutel had depicted him, both in cartoons and speech, as an anti-Semite, a racist, and a Nazi.

New Brunswick Justice Paul Creaghan had no difficulty finding that Ross was an anti-Semite who strongly opposed Judaism and a racist in the sense of opposing racial intermingling. Justice Creaghan said: "[Ross] perceives Judaism as an enemy of traditional Christian teaching.... He embraces and he is prepared to do all he can to defend his faith against a group who he sees as being out to undermine it."

But, Justice Creaghan said, Beutel went beyond the law when he likened Ross to a Nazi — indeed a Nazi propaganda leader (Joseph Goebbels) during the years of Adolf Hitler. Justice Creaghan stated: "[Ross] may have unknowingly, or even knowingly, picked up some ideas from current Nazi sympathizers, but to take as a fact that Malcolm Ross is a Nazi goes too far." Ross was not a member of the Nazi party, and to have stated otherwise, the Justice continued, libeled and defamed him and his reputation. The Justice ordered that Beutel pay Ross $7,500 in damages and $2,000 in court costs (*Toronto Star*, January 20, 2000).

The judgment was appealed to the New Brunswick Court of Appeal. The Canadian Newspaper Association, the Association of Canadian Editorial Cartoonists, the Canadian Jewish Congress, and the League for Human Rights of B'nai Brith Canada joined Beutel's appeal. The appellate court set two days for hearings on the matter.

Douglas Christie, Ross's lawyer, called the groups' interest a "monumental irony." He said: "When Mr. Ross was being denied his job because of deeply held religious beliefs, you didn't hear [many] defending his freedom of speech. But when he is defamed by false and malicious speech, those people proclaim their right to free speech.... [Beutel] mocked Ross's religious beliefs and humiliated him in front of his peers.... The cartoon indicated he was the moral equivalent of Goebbels. It was not true and it was not fair comment."

In a unanimous decision, the New Brunswick Court of Appeal reversed the judgment of the lower court against Beutel. The Chief Justice Joseph Z. Daigle, said, in part: "Honesty in expressing one's real view has been found to be the bedrock foundation for a good defence of fair comment" (*Toronto Star,* June 1, 2001).

THE NATURE OF POLITICAL CARTOONS

Are political cartoons a special kind of expression? In their nature, do they permit exaggeration? We quote in part an editorial by the *Toronto Star* written in response to the judgment of Justice Creaghan in the Ross case action for libel and defamation:

> Love 'em or hate 'em, editorial cartoons of the
> sort that we carry every day on this page are the

lifeblood of democratic politics. Like editorials and opinion columns, they're meant to provoke debate on important social issues. Indeed, more than a few public figures proudly display on their office walls cartoons that have lampooned them.

So it's disturbing that a New Brunswick judge, Mr. Justice Paul Creaghan, has found cartoonist Josh Beutel of the *Saint John Telegraph-Journal* guilty of defaming former teacher Malcolm Ross, by likening him to a Nazi. Beutel was ordered to pay Ross $7,500 in damages for criticizing him at a public forum sponsored by the New Brunswick Teachers' Association, which in turn was ordered to pay Ross $2,100 in court costs....

In a famous judgment on a cartoon that depicted former British Columbia cabinet minister — and later premier — Bill Vander Zalm pulling the wings off a fly, the B.C. appeal court overturned a ruling that the cartoon was libellous because the trial judge failed to take into account "the symbolism, allegory or satire and usual exaggeration to be found in cartoons."

Closer to home, the Ontario Press Council, which serves as a watchdog on press ethics, has long recognized that cartoonists need considerable latitude to ply their art of caricature and exaggeration.

"A cartoonist traditionally uses grotesque representations of persons and things to express controversial, unpopular or satirical opinions on social issues," the council wrote in a judgment last year involving a complaint by the police about a *Toronto Star* cartoon by Patrick Corrigan. In other rulings, the council has found that editorial cartoonists routinely use "caricatures, grotesque representations" and "exaggeration" to make points. "The council's view is that readers do not generally take cartoons literally," it ruled in 1994.

In other words, they know silliness when they see it. Creaghan's judgment flies in the face of common sense and accepted journalistic practice. It risks putting a chill on editorial cartooning. That would undermine free speech and spirited debate in this country. This judgment should be appealed, and overturned (*Toronto Star*, May 4, 1998).

BEYOND THE LAW: A MATTER OF JUDGMENT

In this chapter, we have written about the law and the boundaries imposed on freedom of expression. The essential point here is that the law, declared by legislature, the courts, and the Charter, in effect do no more than set boundaries. How individuals, including the media, respond to those boundaries is another matter.

For example, a Danish publication decided to publish derogatory cartoons of the Prophet Mohammed. This stirred great tension in the Muslim community. There was no doubt that the publisher had the legal right to publish the cartoons. Whether they should have been published was a matter that called for the exercise of individual judgment. Of course, there is nothing to prevent a newspaper or any medium from refusing to publish a matter because in their view it exceeds good taste and fairness (London Free Press, February 13, 2006).

REFERENCES AND FURTHER READING
* Cited by the Supreme Court of Canada.

Globe and Mail."Top Court Rejects Anti-Semite as Teacher." April 4, 1996.

_____. "The Crime, the Proof and the Punishment." April 5, 1996.

Harding, Katherine. "Cartoonist Wins Defamation Case on Appeal." *Toronto Star,* June 1, 2001.

London Free Press. "Editorial Freedom Also Means Responsibility." February 13, 2006.

Reyes, Allison. 1995. "Freedom of Expression and Public School Teachers." *Dalhousie Journal of Legal Studies* 4: 35.*

Statistics Canada, Religions in Canada, Ottawa: Industry, Science and Technology Canada, 1993. 1991 Census Canada, Catalogue No. 93-319.

Toronto Star. "Anti-cartoon Judgment." May 4, 1998.

Toughill, Kelly. "Limits of Free Speech at Stake in Cartoonist's Case." *Toronto Star,* January 20, 2000.

4

CHAPTER 4
FREEDOM OF RELIGION: PLACING LIMITS ON TRADITION

Section 2 of the Charter provides: "Everyone has the following fundamental freedoms: (a) freedom of conscience and religion...." However, section 2(a) is conditioned by section 1 of the Charter: "The Canadian Charter of Rights and Freedoms guarantees the rights and freedoms set out in it subject only to such reasonable limits prescribed by law as can be demonstrably justified in a free and democratic society."

Among the questions raised in this chapter are:

- May public school students claim the right to freedom of religion?
- May the state impose limits on the exercise of freedom of religion?
- Is public safety a reasonable basis for limiting freedom of religion?

The primary case we shall discuss is *Balvir Singh Multani and Balvir Singh Multani, in his capacity as tutor to his minor son, Gurbaj Singh Multani* [Appellants] v. *Commission scolaire Marguerite-Bourgeoys and Attorney General of Quebec* [Respondents] *and* [as Interveners in the case] *World Sikh Organization of Canada,*

Canadian Civil Liberties Association, Canadian Human Rights Commission and Ontario Human Rights Commission. For ease of discussion, we refer to the case as the kirpan case. We refer to the Commission scolaire Marguerite-Bourgeoys as the school board, which it is, in the sense of having supervisory authority over public schools in Quebec.

The kirpan case is concerned not with the right of an adult to freedom of religion, but with that of a minor — a student who claimed the right to wear a kirpan, a symbolic dagger, in the exercise of his religious duties as an Orthodox Sikh. The decision of the Supreme Court of Canada, handed down on March 2, 2006, was unanimous in its conclusion that the student had this right and that the school board had not demonstrated that wearing the kirpan could not be accommodated in the context of school safety.

On the constitutional analysis, Justice Charron spoke for the Court majority. Justices Deschamps and Rosalie Abella would have resolved the issues on non-constitutional grounds. They would have looked to the administrative standard that should have guided the school board, and they would have found that the board interpretation of that standard was unreasonable. Our review of the case is focused on the constitutional analysis of the Court majority.

THE KIRPAN CASE

Gurbaj Singh Multani, twelve, was a public school student in Quebec. Like his father, Balvir Singh Multani, he was baptized as an Orthodox Sikh and believed that his religion required him to wear at all times a kirpan — a twenty-centimeter-long ceremonial dagger with a metal blade, a sheath, and a fabric holster worn close to the body.

On November 19, 2001, the kirpan that Gurbaj Singh was wearing under his clothing (as he usually did) accidentally fell to the ground. The school was concerned that he was carrying something that could injure other students. Its legal counsel sent a letter to Gurbaj Singh's parents authorizing their son to continue wearing the kirpan to school *provided it was sealed inside his clothing.* They agreed with this condition that was seen by them and the school as a "reasonable accommodation."

The school board, however, reached a different conclusion. It refused to ratify the agreement. By resolution, it claimed that the agreement violated regulations issued by it under provincial statutory authority. Included among those regulations was one prohibiting "the carrying of weapons and dangerous objects" on school grounds. The kirpan was viewed as a weapon or dangerous object. On further administrative review by the board, the decision was upheld. However, the reviewing authority stated that it would allow Gurbaj Singh to wear a "symbolic kirpan," one that would be a pendant or that would look like a dagger but would be of a material that would make it harmless.

DECISIONS OF THE LOWER COURTS

Gurbaj Singh (supported by his father) and his father appealed individually the decision of the school board to the Quebec Superior Court. Among other provisions, they cited section 2(a) of the Charter which, as noted, sets out as a fundamental freedom the right to freedom of religion. *At no point did any of the parties question the right of Gurbaj Singh, as a minor and as a student in a public school, to exercise this right.*

Father and son asked the Superior Court to declare invalid the judgment of the school board — and until this was done, they requested an order (called an interim injunction) that would allow Gurbaj Singh to wear his kirpan under the conditions set out in the first letter from school counsel (i.e. sewn under his clothing and sheathed). On April 16, 2002, the interim injunction was allowed on conditions earlier set by the school counsel's letter.

On May 17, 2002, Justice Danielle Grenier of the Superior Court declared the order of the school board null and of no force or effect. The judge authorized Gurbaj Singh to wear the kirpan on the following conditions:

- that it be worn under his clothes;
- that it be carried in a sheath made of wood, not metal, to prevent it from causing injury;
- that it be placed in its sheath and wrapped and sewn in a sturdy cloth envelope, and that this envelope must be sewn to his clothing;
- that school personnel be authorized to verify, in a reasonable fashion, that these conditions were met;
- that Gurbaj Singh keep the kirpan in his possession at all times, and report its disappearance to school authorities immediately;
- that failure to comply with these conditions would result in the loss of Gurbaj Singh's right to wear the kirpan at school.

Justice Grenier discussed first the "accommodation" initially reached between Gurbaj Singh, his parents, and the school. She noted that the need to wear a kirpan was "based on a sincere religious belief held by Gurbaj Singh." And, she found that there was *no evidence of any violent incidents involving kirpans in Quebec schools.*

Her decision was appealed to the Quebec Court of Appeal. Justice Louise Lemelin, speaking for a unanimous court, ruled that the school board had never agreed to "accommodate" Gurbaj Singh. Rather, it had always taken the position that the kirpan must be rendered harmless. The Court of Appeal reversed the decision of Justice Grenier.

For the Court of Appeal, Justice Lemelin had no doubt that Gurbaj Singh's need to wear the kirpan was a sincerely held religious belief — a belief important to him. Nor did she have any doubt that the action taken by the school board infringed on Gurbaj Singh's freedom of religion within the meaning of section 2(a) of the Charter.

The question on appeal was whether the conditions for limiting freedom of religion set out in section 1 of the Charter had been met. The action taken by the school board, she said, "was motivated by a pressing and substantial objective, namely to ensure the safety of the school's students and staff." She stated that there was a direct and rational connection between wearing the kirpan to school and the goal of maintaining a safe environment.

The difficulty with the trial court decision, Justice Lemelin said, was that the kirpan was a dangerous weapon. The conditions imposed by the trial court did not eliminate "every risk." Those conditions only made it more difficult for someone else to pry the weapon from the undergarments of the student. To allow those conditions to stand, she continued, would cause the school board to lower its safety standards. In the result, for the Court of Appeal, she stated that the action taken by the school board was not unreasonable (*Globe and Mail*, April 12, 2005).

THE SUPREME COURT OF CANADA DECIDES

At some point during the litigation, Gurbaj Singh transferred from his public school to a private school where he was permitted to wear the kirpan, consistent with his religious beliefs. The decision of the Quebec Court of Appeal was appealed to the Supreme Court of Canada. Five years after Gurbaj Singh's kirpan had fallen on the grounds of his school, the Supreme Court ruled in his favour. It struck the decision of the school board, and it implied that the conditions first set by school counsel and agreed upon by Gurbaj Singh and his parents probably would meet the requirements of section 1 of the Charter.

Justice Charron, for the Court, spoke of the importance of freedom of religion. She quoted extensively from earlier Court decisions:

> The essence of the concept of freedom of religion
> is the right to entertain such religious beliefs as

a person chooses, the right to declare religious beliefs openly and without fear of hindrance or reprisal, and the right to manifest religious belief by worship and practice or by teaching and dissemination. But the concept means more than that.

Freedom means that, subject to such limitations as are necessary to protect public safety, order, health, or morals or the fundamental rights and freedoms of others, no one is to be forced to act in a way contrary to his beliefs or his conscience....

With the Charter, it has become the right of every Canadian to work out for himself or herself what his or her religious obligations, if any, should be and it is not for the state to dictate otherwise.... Freedom of religion consists ... of the freedom to undertake practices and harbour beliefs, having a nexus [meaningful connection] with religion, in which an individual demonstrates he or she sincerely believes or is sincerely undertaking in order to connect with the divine or as a function of his or her spiritual faith, irrespective of whether a particular practice or belief is required by official religious dogma or is in conformity with the position of religious officials."

The Supreme Court of Canada accepted what the trial and appellate courts had concluded: Wearing the kirpan was an important part of the religious beliefs of Gurbaj Singh. Curtailing his right to wear it impinged on his section 2(a) Charter right to freedom of religion. The burden was on Gurbaj Singh to prove his belief as to wearing the kirpan was important and that it was religiously based. He did that. (For a discussion relating to this, see "You Be the Judge: 'A Religiously Motivated Interpretation,'" below.)

THE PRIMARY ISSUE: SECTION 1 OF THE CHARTER

The school board made its kirpan ruling under authority of a provincial statute. In this sense, the action taken was that of government. *For this reason, that action had to conform with the Charter.* The action was a rule of law within the meaning of section 1 of the Charter which guarantees the rights and freedoms set out in it subject only to such reasonable limits prescribed by law as can be demonstrably justified in a free and democratic society.

The burden of proof was on the school board to show, on a balance of probabilities, that the infringement was reasonable and demonstrably could be justified in a free and democratic society (the language of section 1). This required the board to meet two standards:

1. The kirpan rule must be sufficiently important to limit a constitutional right.
2. The means chosen by the school board must be proportional to the purpose of the rule. (That is, the rule must do no more than is necessary to achieve a legitimate government objective.)

Justice Charron examined the *objective of the kirpan rule.* She quoted from the Court of Appeal decision which stated that the board's ruling "was motivated by [a pressing and substantial] objective, namely, to ensure an environment conducive to the development and learning of the students. This requires [the board] to ensure the safety of the students and the staff. This duty is at the core of the mandate entrusted to educational institutions."

Gurbaj Singh conceded that this was a proper objective and that it passed the first stage of the test. The board also submitted fairly detailed evidence consisting of affidavits from various stakeholders in the educational community explaining the importance of safety in schools and the upsurge in problems relating to weapons and violence in schools.

Yet, Justice Charron said that *the board's goal, while valid, had to be more fully defined*:

> Clearly, the objective of ensuring safety in schools is sufficiently important to warrant overriding a constitutionally protected right or freedom. It remains to be determined what level of safety the governing board was seeking to achieve by prohibiting the carrying of weapons and dangerous objects, and what degree of risk would accordingly be tolerated.... The possibilities range from a desire to ensure absolute safety to a total lack of concern for safety. Between these two extremes lies a concern to ensure a reasonable level of safety.

On the facts, Justice Charron found that the goal of the school board was to achieve *reasonable safety in the schools*. This was a goal that fell between *absolute safety* and *minimal safety*. (For a discussion of this, see "A Matter of Balance," below.) And, such a goal, she said is, without question, a pressing and substantial one.

PROPORTIONALITY

In her section 1 analysis, Justice Charron moved to the issue of proportionality. This relates to the means used to achieve a proper goal — in this instance, reasonable safety in the schools. Here the question is: *Does the board's kirpan rule further its goal of reasonable safety in the schools?* She said such a connection existed:

> Prohibiting Gurbaj Singh from wearing his kirpan to school was intended to further this objective [of reasonable safety in the schools]. Despite the profound religious significance of the kirpan for Gurbaj Singh, it also has the characteristics

of a bladed weapon and could therefore cause injury. The [board's] decision therefore has a rational connection with the objective of ensuring a reasonable level of safety in schools. Moreover, it is relevant that [Gurbaj Singh] has never contested the rationality of the ... rule prohibiting weapons in school.

The next issue under proportionality is one that often is central to whether the questioned action can be justified under section 1 of the Charter. The Supreme Court has ruled that *the limit must minimally impair the right or freedom that has been violated.* Yet, this does not mean, said Justice Charron, that the "impairment" be the least possible invasion. This is how she expressed the standard: "The impairment must be 'minimal,' that is, the law must be carefully tailored so that rights are impaired no more than necessary. The tailoring process seldom admits of perfection and the courts must accord some leeway to the legislator. If the law falls within a range of reasonable alternatives, the courts will not find it overbroad merely because they can conceive of an alternative which might better tailor objective to infringement."

This is the standard to apply to the school board in the kirpan case. Justice Charron stated: "It must be determined whether the decision to establish an absolute prohibition against wearing a kirpan 'falls within a range of reasonable alternatives.'"

Yet, what the school board did was to impose an absolute prohibition against Gurbaj Singh wearing his kirpan to school. It claimed this was necessary because the presence of the kirpan at the school would pose numerous risks for the school's pupils and staff. Yet, said Justice Charron, it was important to note that Gurbaj Singh never claimed a right to wear his kirpan to school without restrictions. Rather, he was willing to accept conditions imposed by Grenier J. of the Superior Court.

THE BOARD'S ARGUMENTS

Justice Charron summarized the board's fears, and then proceeded to deal with each of them:

- To allow the kirpan to be worn to school involves the risk that it could be used for violent purposes by the person wearing it, or by another student who might take it away from him.
- It could lead to an increase in the number of weapons at the school.
- Its presence could have a negative impact on the school environment. The board argued that the kirpan is a symbol of violence and that it sends the message that the use of force is a way to assert rights and resolve conflicts. This, in turn, would undermine the sense of safety and compromise the spirit of fairness that should prevail in schools, in that its presence suggests the existence of a double standard.

Bear in mind that Justice Charron's approach to each board argument was in reference to the objective or legitimate Charter goal of *establishing reasonable safety in the school — not absolute safety.* For the Court, she stated that the evidence showed that Gurbaj Singh did not have behavioural problems. Nor had he ever resorted to violence at school. Further, Justice Charron said:

> The risk that this particular student would use his kirpan for violent purposes seems highly unlikely to me. In fact, the [board] has never argued that there was a risk of his doing so.
>
> As for the risk of another student taking his kirpan away from him, it also seems to me to be quite low, especially if the kirpan is worn under

conditions such as were imposed by Grenier J. of the Superior Court. In the instant case, if the kirpan were worn in accordance with those conditions, any student wanting to take it away from Gurbaj Singh would first have to physically restrain him, then search through his clothes, remove the sheath from his guthra, and try to unstitch or tear open the cloth enclosing the sheath in order to get to the kirpan. There is no question that a student who wanted to commit an act of violence could find another way to obtain a weapon, such as bringing one in from outside the school. Furthermore, there are many objects in schools that could be used to commit violent acts and that are much more easily obtained by students, such as scissors, pencils and baseball bats.

In her brief reasons, Grenier J. explained that her decision was based in part on the fact that "the evidence revealed no instances of violent incidents involving kirpans in schools in Quebec" and on "the state of Canadian and American law on this matter." In fact, the evidence in the record suggests that, over the 100 years since Sikhs have been attending schools in Canada, not a single violent incident related to the presence of kirpans in schools has been reported.

The lack of evidence of risks related to the wearing of kirpans was also noted in 1990 by a board of inquiry of the Ontario Human Rights Commission, which considered the presence of kirpans in schools in great depth in *Pandori v. Peel Board of Education* (1990), 12 *Canadian Human Rights Reports* D/364; its decision was affirmed by the Ontario Divisional Court in *Peel School*

Board v. Ontario Human Rights Commission
(1991), 3 *Ontario Reports* (3d series) 531, and
leave to appeal was refused by the Ontario Court
of Appeal. The board of inquiry allowed kirpans
to be worn in Ontario schools under conditions
similar to the ones imposed by Grenier J. of the
Quebec Superior Court. The board noted that
there had been no incidents involving kirpans in
Canadian schools....

The decision was affirmed by the Ontario
Divisional Court, which stated: "We can see no
error in principle in the way it applied its judgment to the facts of this case, particularly in light
of the lack of any incident of kirpan-related violence in any school system [in Canada]."

Justice Charron, reviewing the evidence, found no basis for any
claim that kirpans had been used as weapons in schools. Yet, there
remained the claim of the board that it did not have to wait for harm
to be done before acting. However, she said, that fear, not founded on
fact, would not satisfy the burden placed on the board by section 1 of
the Charter to *justify an infringement of Gurbaj Singh's right to freedom of religion.* She said: "Given the evidence in the record, it is my
opinion that the [board's] argument in support of an absolute prohibition — namely that kirpans are inherently dangerous — must fail."
There remained, however, two other board arguments:

1. Allowing kirpans would encourage students to bring other
   weapons to school.
2. The mere presence of kirpans would "contribute to a poison-
   ing of the school environment."

Justice Charron analyzed and dismissed both arguments.
As to the first claim, she said it was essentially covered in her

review of the lack of any evidence that kirpans had been used as weapons in schools. There simply was no evidence that students wearing kirpans acted as a motivator for other students to arm themselves. She concluded that the argument, in effect, was "purely speculative."

Finally, there was the claim on the part of the board that allowing kirpans would have a negative impact on school environment. It would substitute the symbol of violence or force for peaceful resolution of disputes. Justice Charron rejected the argument not only because it was contradicted by the evidence, but also because, in the view of the Court, it did "not take into account Canadian values based on multiculturalism." She wrote: "Religious tolerance is a very important value of Canadian society. If some students consider it unfair that Gurbaj Singh may wear his kirpan to school while they are not allowed to have knives in their possession, it is incumbent on the schools to discharge their obligation to instill in their students this value that is, as I will explain in the next section, at the very foundation of our democracy. "

In the result, Gurbaj Singh's right to wear a kirpan, under conditions, was affirmed. However, as noted, at some point during the appeal process, he left the public school system and entered a private school which permitted students to wear the kirpan.

Justice Charron, for the Court, was not required to enter an order relating specifically to Gurbaj Singh. The Court did enter an order that declared the board rule void. But, the reasoning beyond that order clearly suggested that the conditions first imposed by the trial court relating to wearing the kirpan would be allowed (*Globe and Mail,* March 3, 2006).

YOU BE THE JUDGE

"A RELIGIOUSLY MOTIVATED INTERPRETATION"

THE FACTS

The facts that follow were suggested in the kirpan case.

Randy Smith, a bright and alert fifteen-year-old, has become interested in Sikhism. His parents, who are non-religious, have done nothing to dissuade him. They see him as capable of making up his own mind.

With his parents' permission, Randy has attended a number of Sikh meetings. He has studied Sikh scriptures, and firmly and fully embraces the tenets of Sikhism, including the wearing of the kirpan. He keeps the kirpan on his body at all times. Yet, he has not formally become a Sikh; he has not been baptized as such. He would like to change his name to include that which Sikh men are called: "singh," meaning lion.

Randy is enrolled in a British Columbia public high school. There have been incidents of violence between students on school grounds. Weapons of many kinds have been used in such fights, including guns and knives. For many years the school board has had a policy prohibiting anyone entering school grounds from carrying guns or knives. They are considered dangerous weapons. Kirpans, from the viewpoint of the school board, fall into this category.

However, the school board, following discussions with representatives of the Sikh community, has modified its policy relating to kirpans: If the student is in fact a Sikh, he will be permitted to carry a kirpan in school. However, it must be sheathed and not visible, and it must be sewn to his clothing.

But, the school board does not consider Randy to be a Sikh. The fact that he sincerely believes in the tenets of Sikhim is not relevant. Under no circumstances will he be permitted, regardless of his wishes, to wear a kirpan under the school board's kirpan exception.

THE ISSUE

May Randy claim the right to freedom of religion within the meaning of section 2(a) of the Charter and carry the Sikh kirpan?

POINTS TO CONSIDER

- The burden of proof is on Randy to show that his convictions are based on religion.
- Randy must demonstrate that the position of the school board is not a "trivial" interference with his ability to act in accordance with his religious beliefs.
- Randy has not formally been baptized into the Sikh religion.
- By far, the majority of males in the Sikh community in the area where Randy lives agree with the school board policy concerning kirpans.
- Randy's religious belief concerning the wearing of the kirpan on the outer part of his clothing is sincere.
- It is a general rule of law that the trial court judge makes findings as to the credibility of

witnesses (that is, as to whether they are to be believed, a finding often based on demeanour).

DISCUSSION

The issue is preliminary to the question as to whether the school board rule is reasonable in meeting the conditions set out in section 1 of the Charter. *Unless Randy can satisfy the test of religious convictions, he cannot challenge the reasonableness of the school board rule.* He must first prove that he is motivated by sincerely-held religious convictions. If he cannot do this, then the school board rule cannot be challenged by him on grounds that it violates his freedom of religion under section 2(a) of the Charter.

Justice Charron, speaking for the majority in the kirpan case, cited earlier Supreme Court of Canada decisions and stated that freedom of religion allows individuals the freedom to follow their religious practices or beliefs regardless of whether or not they conform with official religious dogma. To establish that their freedom of religion has been infringed, individuals must demonstrate sincere belief that their practices or beliefs have a real connection with religion and that a serious attempt has been made to interfere with their ability to act in accordance with those practices or beliefs.

WHAT WAS PROVED IN THE KIRPAN CASE
Now, compare what the student proved in the kirpan case as compared to this exercise. We will deal first with the kirpan case. Here, what the student attempted to prove was that his faith required him at all times to wear a kirpan made

of metal. Evidence was introduced, which was not contradicted. No one contested the fact that the orthodox Sikh religion requires its adherents to wear a kirpan at all times.

Viewing the evidence, Justice Charron stated:

> The affidavits of [Sikh] chaplain
> Manjit Singh and of Gurbaj Singh [the
> student] explain that Orthodox Sikhs must
> comply with a strict dress code requiring
> them to wear religious symbols commonly
> known as the Five Ks: (1) the kesh (uncut
> hair); (2) the kangha (a wooden comb);
> (3) the kara (a steel bracelet worn on the
> wrist); (4) the kaccha (a special undergar-
> ment); and (5) the kirpan (a metal dagger or
> sword). Furthermore, Manjit Singh explains
> in his affidavit that the Sikh religion teaches
> pacifism and encourages respect for other
> religions, that the kirpan must be worn at
> all times, even in bed, that it must not be
> used as a weapon to hurt anyone, and that
> Gurbaj Singh's refusal to wear a symbolic
> kirpan made of a material other than metal
> is based on a *reasonable religiously moti-
> vated interpretation* [emphasis added].

For the Court, Justice Charron ruled:

> The fact that different people practise the
> same religion in different ways does not
> affect the validity of the case of a person
> alleging that his or her freedom of religion

has been infringed. What an individual must do is show that he or she sincerely believes that a certain belief or practice is required by his or her religion. The religious belief must be asserted in good faith and must not be fictitious, capricious or an artifice.... In assessing the sincerity of the belief, a court must take into account, *inter alia* [among other things], the credibility of the testimony of the person asserting the particular belief and the consistency of the belief with his or her other current religious practices... .

[The student] says that he sincerely believes he must adhere to this practice in order to comply with the requirements of his religion. Grenier J. of the Superior Court declared ... and the Court of Appeal reached the same conclusion ... that [the student's] belief was sincere. [The student's] affidavit supports this conclusion, and none of the parties have contested the sincerity of his belief.

Furthermore, [the student's] refusal to wear a replica made of a material other than metal is not capricious. He genuinely believes that he would not be complying with the requirements of his religion were he to wear a plastic or wooden kirpan. *The fact that other Sikhs accept such a compromise is not relevant, since as [the trial judge] mentioned in her decision, "We must recognize that people who profess the same religion may adhere to the dogma and practices of that religion to varying degrees of rigour* [emphasis added]."

Finally, the interference with [the student's] freedom of religion is neither trivial nor insignificant. Forced to choose between leaving his kirpan at home and leaving the public school system, [he] decided to follow his religious convictions and is now attending a private school. The prohibition against wearing his kirpan to school has therefore deprived him of his right to attend a public school.

WHAT RANDY MUST PROVE

On the facts, there are similarities between Randy and the student in the kirpan case. Both profess belief in that part of Sikhism which requires the wearing of what the Supreme Court of Canada referred to as the "Five Ks," including the kirpan. Both were minors, and both had asserted their religious beliefs while they were attending a public school. Both were subject to school rules which prohibited anyone from bringing to the school dangerous weapons, including daggers.

But, on the facts — and, ultimately, on the law — there are some differences between the two students. In the kirpan case, the student had been baptized, that is, formally initiated into the Sikh religion. Further, he had (among others) the chaplain of the temple where he prayed testify in his behalf as to his belief in the kirpan, and its importance

— and whether it should be a real dagger, made of metal, or something smaller, made perhaps of wood or plastic.

Randy has never formally been baptized into the Sikh faith. Nor does he have anyone to testify for him — other than perhaps his parents — concerning his adherence to Sikh tenets. But, Justice Charron made it clear that being a formal member of a religion is not a pre-condition to the exercise of a claim to freedom of religion under section 2(a) of the Charter.

Still, the fact that Randy merely says that he believes in carrying the kirpan as a religious duty does not necessarily make it possible for him to do so. Justice Charron said that the claim to religious belief must be sincere and that it must reflect a deeply held belief. And, what this comes to is a matter of credibility. That is, *Randy must convince the trial court judge, just as was done in the kirpan case, that he really means what he says.* In the kirpan case, there was, in addition to the testimony of the student, the evidence of others, including a Sikh chaplain, who spoke about the nature of the Sikh religion and, as importantly, about the student's "reasonable interpretation" of the kirpan requirement.

One can only say, again on the facts, that in law the decision as to whether Randy is credible will be left to the trial judge. It is the trial judge who must decide whether to believe or doubt whether Randy really holds as a religious conviction that carrying a kirpan of the kind described is necessary to his religious beliefs. But, it should be added, even if Randy satisfies the judge on this point, there remains the question, central to our discussion of the kirpan case, as to *whether the school board rule was reasonable.*

CHALLENGE QUESTION

KIRPANS ON PLANES?

Air Canada announced a rule that kirpans, along with other sharp instruments, would not be permitted on any of its flights, either domestic or foreign. This was an absolute rule. No exceptions would be allowed.

Q. The issue was presented to a Canadian Human Rights Tribunal which administers a law that includes prohibiting religious discrimination. Should the rule in the kirpan case be applied? That is, should Air Canada be required to justify its rule in terms of "minimal impairment" of the right of Sikhs who believe, as an article of religious faith, that they must carry kirpans? In effect, is this case similar to that which the Supreme Court decided as to Sikh students in public schools?

Justice Charron discussed this issue in the kirpan case. She quoted from the tribunal's decision allowing the Air Canada rule to stand. The tribunal stated (and Justice Charron apparently agreed):

> In assessing whether or not [Air Canada's] weapons policy can be modified so as to accommodate Sikhs detrimentally affected, consideration must be given to the environment in which the rule must be applied. *In this regard, we are satisfied that aircraft present a unique environment. Groups of strangers are brought together and are required to stay together, in confined spaces,*

for prolonged periods of time. Emergency medical and police assistance are not readily accessible [emphasis added].

Unlike the school environment ... where there is an ongoing relationship between the student and the school and with that a meaningful opportunity to assess the circumstances of the individual seeking the accommodation, air travel involves a transitory population. Significant numbers of people are processed each day, with minimal opportunity for assessment. It will be recalled that Mr. Kinnear testified that Canada 3000 check-in personnel have between 45 and 90 seconds of contact with each passenger.

A KIRPAN IN A COURTROOM?

Question: May a judge ban kirpans in a courtroom? Is this really any different than a school prohibiting kirpans?
Answer: Justice Charron dealt with this question. In the kirpan case, it was raised by the school board as a justification for prohibiting the use of kirpans. The case was *The Queen v. Hothi*, [1985] 3 *Western Weekly Reports* 256 (Manitoba Court of Queen's Bench), affirmed on appeal, [1986] 3 *Western Weekly Reports* 671 (Manitoba Court of Appeal).

The trial judge was permitted to impose a no-kirpan rule. But, Justice Charron noted what she called the "special circumstances" of the case. She said:

The judge who prohibited the wearing of the kirpan in the courtroom was hearing the case of an accused charged with assault under §245 of the Criminal Code. [The judge noted] the special nature of courts and stated the following about wearing kirpans in courtrooms: "It serves a transcending public interest that justice be administered in an environment free from any influence which may tend to thwart the process [of justice]. Possession in the courtroom of weapons, or articles capable of use as such, by parties of others is one such influence." [Justice Charron seemed to agree with this statement.]

A MATTER OF BALANCE

In the kirpan case, the Supreme Court of Canada ruled that an absolute ban on the kirpan in schools was not a *reasonable limit* within the meaning of section 1 of the Charter. However, let's assume that the Court accepted that the kirpan ban was a reasonable means for achieving school safety.

Section 1 of the Charter would still require that a determination as to *whether the harmful effects of allowing the kirpan outweigh its positive effects.* And, Justice Charron suggested that *the negative effects of prohibiting the use of the kirpan would outweigh the positive effects of promoting school safety.* In her statement, she included citations of past Supreme Court of Canada decisions and stated:

An absolute prohibition would stifle the promotion of values such as multiculturalism, diversity, and the development of an educational culture respectful of the rights of others. This Court has on numerous occasions reiterated the importance of these values. For example [she said, citing other Supreme Court of Canada decisions]:

"A school is a communication centre for a whole range of values and aspirations of a society. In large part, it defines the values that transcend society through the educational medium. The school is an arena for the exchange of ideas and must, therefore, be premised upon principles of tolerance and impartiality so that all persons within the school environment feel equally free to participate.

"Schools ... have a duty to foster the respect of their students for the constitutional rights of all members of society. Learning respect for those rights is essential to our democratic society and should be part of the education of all students. These values are best taught by example and may be undermined if the students' rights are ignored by those in authority.

"Our Court [has] accepted that teachers are a medium for the transmission of values.... Schools are meant to develop civic virtue and responsible citizenship, to educate in an environment free of bias, prejudice and intolerance."

Justice Charron continued:

A total prohibition against wearing a kirpan to school undermines the value of this religious symbol and sends students the message that some religious practices do not merit the same protection as others. On the other hand, accommodating [the student] and allowing him to wear his kirpan under certain conditions demonstrates the importance that our society attaches to protecting freedom of religion and to showing respect for its minorities. The deleterious effects of a total prohibition thus outweigh its salutary [positive] effects.

YOU BE THE JUDGE

THE CASE OF "ZERO TOLERANCE"

This case is a hypothetical one. It serves to illustrate points of law.

THE FACTS

Violence has been rampant in the public high schools administered by the Runnymede School Board of British Columbia. The intensity of that violence has steadily increased over the past four years. There have been numerous injuries to students, and even to some teachers who have tried to end fights. Several of these injuries have been life-threatening.

The weapons of choice range from handguns to knives and sharp instruments (such as compasses) used in studies. Fighting has taken place in the school and on school grounds, both during and after school hours.

Police and school investigators have been an increasing presence. Their investigations have pointed to a number of causes including gang development and competition, drugs, and a resulting "culture of violence."

The school board, an elected body governed by statute, has responsibility to "ensure the safety of students and school staff so that an environment conducive to learning can be maintained."

The board has held a number of meetings open to the public, and especially to parents, students, and staff of its high schools. Board officials have been there to answer questions, interact, and receive suggestions. By far, the suggestion approved by most was put forward by students, themselves: *zero tolerance.* That is, *absolutely no instrument that could be used to fight should be permitted. And, fighting, itself, was to be banned.*

The board accepts the proposal. Metal detectors are placed throughout each public high school. Everyone coming onto school grounds is subject to search by school officials or police (who are invited onto school grounds by the board for that purpose). Any sharp instrument, including compasses or scissors, will be confiscated and will not be returned. Any student who has material confiscated twice will be subject to discipline, including suspension. As for fighting, those involved even in a first offence will be subject to a one-week suspension, and this penalty could be increased (up to and including expulsion), depending on the severity of the fight and resulting injuries.

Raul Singh, like Gurbaj Singh Multani in the kirpan case, is an Orthodox Sikh. As a religious matter, he believes it is absolutely necessary for him to have a kirpan. Unlike Gurbaj Singh, he is absolutely unwilling to have the dagger sealed in cloth and sewn to the inside of his clothing. Yet, like Gurbaj Singh, he strongly believes that his religion forbids the use of the dagger as a weapon.

For its part, the school board is firm and clear as to its policy: The kirpan cannot be taken to school under any circumstances. It is a dagger, and the school board has a rule of zero tolerance.

THE ISSUES

- Under the Charter and its provision for religious freedom of belief, is the school board authorized to issue a zero-tolerance rule for the high schools subject to its regulations?
- What is the effect of Raul Singh's religious beliefs on the validity of the zero-tolerance rule?

POINTS TO CONSIDER

- The Charter of Rights and Freedoms is part of the Constitution of Canada and, as such, it is the supreme law of the land.
- Section 2(a) of the Charter provides that "everyone has ... freedom of conscience and religion."
- There is no question that Raul Singh wears a kirpan as a matter of religious belief.
- Nor is there any question that the same religious belief compels Raul Singh to refuse to sew and hide the kirpan under his clothes.
- If the zero-tolerance rule does violate Raul Singh's right to freedom of religion, the school board may attempt to justify its action under section 1 of the Charter.
- Such justification must demonstrate that the rule is sufficiently important to warrant limiting the right to freedom of religion.
- And, the justification under section 1 of the Charter also requires that the means chosen by the school board be reasonably related (proportional) to the objective of the rule.

DISCUSSION

The general facts of this section were alluded to by Justice Charron, who wrote the majority opinion in the kirpan case. The start point in analysis is that Raul Singh's right to freedom of religion has been violated under section 2(a) of the Charter. He has a sincere religious belief regarding the kirpan that may or may not have been endorsed by his religion. But, whatever other Sikhs might believe concerning the kirpan, it does not take away from Raul Singh's right to assert his belief.

The real issues for resolving the case centre on whether the school was justified in its actions under section 1 of the Charter. There are three aspects to a likely decision:

1. Was the objective of the zero-tolerance rule important relative to the proper objectives of the school board?
2. If the rule objective was proper, were the means chosen (the rule procedures) proportional? That is, did the means go beyond the legitimate thrust of the rule?
3. What should be the nature of the remedy, if any?

The burden of justifying the violation of Raul Singh's right to freedom of religion is on the school board. In the kirpan case, Justice Charron stated:

> The onus is on the [school board] to prove that, on a balance of probabilities, the infringement is reasonable and can be demonstrably justified in a free and democratic society. To this end, two requirements must be met. First, the legislative objective being pursued must be

sufficiently important to warrant limiting a constitutional right. Next, the means chosen by the state authority must be proportional to the objective in question."

We will examine each of these aspects.

OBJECTIVE OF THE ZERO-TOLERANCE RULE

The stated objective of the school board was to obtain safety in the high schools. This was the same objective of the school board in the kirpan case. And, it was an objective strong enough to override a claim to freedom of religion under the Charter. Justice Charron said in the kirpan case:

> [The board's] decision was motivated by [a pressing and substantial] objective, namely, to ensure an environment conducive to the development and learning of the students. This requires [the board] to ensure the safety of the students and the staff. This duty is at the core of the mandate entrusted to educational institutions. The appellant concedes that this objective is laudable and that it passes the first stage of the [section 1] test. The [school board] also submitted fairly detailed evidence consisting of affidavits from various stakeholders in the educational community explaining the importance of safety in schools and the upsurge in problems relating to weapons and violence in schools.

Clearly, the objective of ensuring safety in schools is sufficiently important to warrant overriding a constitutionally protected right or freedom.

OBJECTIVE DEFINED

This hypothetical case presents an *absolute* rule. It is a rule of zero tolerance. No exceptions are allowed under the rule. The purpose of the rule is to approximate *absolute safety*. Justice Charron suggested in the kirpan case that such an objective might be beyond the scope of a school board's legitimate objectives, taken by the Court as *providing universal access to the public school system*. In the kirpan case, Justice Charron said that *the school board did not want to attempt absolute safety. It wanted to achieve reasonable safety.* And, this was appropriate. The means used to achieve this objective could be measured. She stated:

> It remains to be determined what level of safety the governing board was seeking to achieve by prohibiting the carrying of weapons and dangerous objects, and what degree of risk would accordingly be tolerated.... The possibilities range from a desire to ensure absolute safety to a total lack of concern for safety. Between these two extremes lies a concern to ensure a reasonable level of safety.
>
> Although the parties did not present argument on the level of safety sought by the governing board, the issue was addressed

by the intervener Canadian Human Rights Commission, which correctly stated that the standard that seems to be applied in schools is reasonable safety, not absolute safety. The application of a standard of absolute safety could result in the installation of metal detectors in schools, the prohibition of all potentially dangerous objects (such as scissors, compasses, baseball bats and table knives in the cafeteria) and permanent expulsion from the public school system of any student exhibiting violent behaviour. Apart from the fact that such a standard would be impossible to attain, it would compromise the objective of providing universal access to the public school system.

On the other hand, when the governing board [initially] approved the article in question, it was not seeking to establish a minimum standard of safety. As can be seen from the affidavits of certain stakeholders from the educational community, violence and weapons are not tolerated in schools, and students exhibiting violent or dangerous behaviour are punished. Such measures show that the objective is to attain a certain level of safety beyond a minimum threshold.

I therefore conclude that the level of safety chosen by the governing council and confirmed by the council of commissioners was reasonable safety. The objective of ensuring a reasonable level of safety in schools is without question a pressing and substantial one.

In this sense, the school board in the kirpan case acted properly. Its rule was intended to help establish *reasonable safety.*

What was said in the kirpan case could not be stated in this hypothetical case. In both cases, the general objective of safety in the schools was appropriate. However, in the hypothetical case, the rule was too inclusive relative to the legitimate objectives of the school board. The rule was designed to achieve *absolute safety.* This, the Court in the kirpan case suggested, was beyond the power of the school board in terms of the outer boundary that would be allowed by the Charter.

But, the school board rule, as applied in the kirpan case, failed the section 1 test of the Charter for another reason: The school board, which carried the burden of proof, did not show that its rule was crafted to minimally impair the religious rights of the student in the pursuit of reasonable school safety.

THE REMEDY

At the time of judgment in the kirpan case, the student no longer attended the school which had banned daggers. What remedy, then, was to be ordered? Justice Charron noted the power given the Court under section 24(1) of the Charter: "Anyone whose rights or freedoms, as guaranteed by this Charter, have been infringed or denied may apply to a court of competent jurisdiction to obtain such remedy as the court considers appropriate and just in the circumstances."

The remedy ordered in the kirpan case was simply to declare the decision prohibiting the student from wearing his kirpan to be "null."

What would be the probable outcome in this hypothetical situation? The student (or others similarly situated, if the case were brought as a class action) would be subject to the school board rule until the Court declared it void. But, in all likelihood, that would not be the end of the matter. The Court had declared that there is a zone for proper board action to provide for reasonable school safety. The school board would not be precluded from enacting such a rule — and, of course, having it tested under the conditions set by section 1 of the Charter.

CHALLENGE QUESTION

A POLL, PUBLIC OPINION, AND THE CHARTER

Q. Should public opinion be a factor in determining the outcome of a religious freedom question under the Canadian Charter of Rights and Freedoms?

After what we have called the kirpan case was decided, the *Globe and Mail* conducted an online poll. On March 3, 2006, it asked: "Do you agree with the Supreme Court decision permitting Sikh students to carry ceremonial daggers in school?" There were more than 20,000 responses. Of these, 5,372 agreed with the Court's decision (26 percent). However, 15,460 disagreed with the Court's ruling (74 percent).

At one level, the answer is quite straightforward. Courts are to be independent, and judges are to apply law to facts. That is part of what makes a society civilized. But, at another level, the question becomes more complex. We see ourselves as a democratic society. Parliament and provincial legislatures, within their areas of authority, are supreme. And, our legislators are responsive to the people. So, if the people give voice through their legislators that they do not like a particular rule of law as handed down by a court, then why can't the legislature overturn that rule and declare, through law, a new rule? Why couldn't provincial legislature simply declare as law: No student may carry any weapon, such as a dagger, regardless of that person's religious beliefs?

The answer has two parts:

1. Government is not entirely free to declare and have enforced whatever it desires. Government is subject to the Charter of Rights and Freedoms, which is part of the Constitution of Canada and, as such, is the supreme law of the land. The Charter, in section 2(a), provides that everyone has the right to *freedom of religion*. It was that *constitutional right* that the Supreme Court of Canada was called upon to interpret in the kirpan case. The Court's interpretation thus has become the *supreme law of the land.*

2. However, the same Charter does permit a legislature (either the Parliament or a provincial legislature) to declare that it will *operate notwithstanding rights set out in sections 2 and 7 to 15.* But, to do this, the legislature must be specific in its language and its intent. And, any such law will be in effect for only five years (unless the legislature earlier revokes it). Further, a

legislature may "re-enact" the "notwithstanding law" at the end of the statutory period.

This is a legislative exception designed to be used sparingly by legislatures. Thus, as applied to the kirpan case, it is *possible for a legislature to override the Supreme Court's decision.* But, this would have to be in the form of a new and a specific law that makes such an override clear. The new law, initially, would last for a maximum of five years, unless it were re-enacted. (These conditions are set out in section 33 of the Charter.)

ALBERTA: DRIVER'S LICENCES AND HUTTERITE CONCERNS

Here the discussion centres not so much on the positive right to speak or to express oneself by dress. Rather, the discussion centres on the *right to be left alone.*

The religious convictions of Hutterites are deeply held. Their religion is central to their lives. For the most part, they live together in colonies. It is the colony (or commune) that holds property and assigns work. So far as possible, they live apart from larger communities.

While they live in a communal environment, the facts, agreed to by the government, are that the Hutterites are quite independent. They do not ask for help from "outsiders."

To a considerable extent, Hutterite convictions are founded on the Ten Commandments. Their religion, started in Switzerland in the sixteenth century and initially rooted in Europe and Russia, is pacifist. In part, their refusal to join the armies of the Czar led to their persecution and flight to Canada and the United States. They established colonies in Alberta, Saskatchewan, and British Columbia, and also in Montana, Washington, and North and

South Dakota. (According to census data, there were about 3,500 Hutterites resident in Alberta in 2001.)

An important part of the Hutterites' belief system includes the Second Commandment, "Thou shalt not make unto thee any graven image." To some Hutterites, this means no images of God. But, it has also been interpreted to include no taking of photographs or posing for them. The reasoning seems to be that humans are created in the image of God.

DRIVER'S LICENCES

For twenty-nine years, the government of Alberta allowed driver's licences to be issued to resident Hutterites without any identifying photos.

For Hutterites, driving is not a recreational matter. Certain individuals are assigned work that may include driving. For example, drivers might be needed to go into the cities for supplies or to obtain medical services for other Hutterites, including children.

In 2003 the agency charged with auto licence registration issued new rules requiring photos of those licensed. Approximately two hundred and fifty Hutterites who held licences without photos at that time lost their exemption.

The agency explained the purpose of the compulsory photo requirement: It was designed to prevent identity theft in relation to auto licensing. The agency showed that identity theft was a growing problem. However, the agency could point to only a single case of identity theft in relation to licensing, and that did not involve a Hutterite.

Under the new regulation, photo identification was placed in a digital depository and retrieved to show whether the person photographed was indeed the person who obtained the licence. The retrieval was not foolproof, but it had a factual basis. The photo on the licence could be compared on a one-to-one basis with the photo on deposit, and it could be compared with those with similar features.

The agency was sensitive to the concerns and beliefs of the Hutterites. Before the regulation came into force, the agency and Hutterite representatives met. The agency made offers to partially shield the showing of any photographed Hutterite auto licencee. In part, this would have been done by storing the digital photo in the depository and not on the licence itself. The compromise was not acceptable to the Hutterites.

THE SUPREME COURT DECIDES

The matter came before the Supreme Court of Canada. The issue was clear: Government, by law (regulation), had infringed upon the Hutterite freedom of conscience and religion. The Court had to decide whether that infringement, in the words of section 1 of the Charter, *was a reasonable limit prescribed by law as can be demonstrably justified in a free and democratic society.*

By a 4–3 vote, the Supreme Court ruled the regulation lawful under the Charter (*Alberta v. Hutterian Brethren of Wilson Colony,* [2009] *Supreme Court of Canada Cases* 37). Chief Justice McLachlin wrote the majority opinion, and Justice Abella wrote a lengthy dissent that also gave rise to other dissenting opinions endorsing her statement of principles.

The burden of the government, said the chief justice, was to show that the photo regulation was rationally connected to a "pressing and substantial goal" and that it minimally impaired the Hutterites' freedom of religion. In this regard, the goal and the minimal impairment are to be balanced to ensure that the regulation is proportionate in its effects.

The chief justice said that the goal of the agency (mandatory photo identification) met a real concern, namely identity theft, and that it was a reasonable approach. It was not for the Court, she continued, to substitute its judgment as to the most reasonable approach for that of the administrative agency.

Section 1 of the Charter, the chief justice said, requires

balancing the legitimate interests of the state against the encroached guaranteed freedom of religion of the Hutterites. She found the encroachment on the Hutterites to be minimal and the legitimate goal of the state (identity theft) to be substantial. She wrote:

> The law has an important social goal — to maintain an effective driver's licence scheme that minimizes the risk of fraud to citizens as a whole. This is not a goal that should lightly be sacrificed. The evidence supports the conclusion that the universal photo requirement addresses a pressing problem and will reduce the risk of identity-related fraud, when compared to a photo requirement that permits exceptions.
>
> Against this important public benefit must be weighed the impact of the limit on the claimants' religious rights. While the limit imposes costs in terms of money and inconvenience as the price of maintaining the religious practice of not submitting to photos, it does not deprive members of their ability to live in accordance with their beliefs. Its deleterious [hurtful] effects, while not trivial, fall at the less serious end of the scale.
>
> Balancing the salutary [positive] and deleterious [harmful] effects of the law, I conclude that the impact of the limit on religious practice associated with the universal photo requirement for obtaining a driver's licence, is proportionate.
>
> I conclude that the limit on the Colony members' freedom of religion imposed by the universal photo requirement for holders of driver's licences has been shown to be justified under section 1 of the Charter. The goal of minimizing the risk of fraud associated with driver's licences is pressing

and substantial. The limit is rationally connected to the goal. The limit impairs the right as little as reasonably possible in order to achieve the goal; the only alternative proposed would significantly compromise the goal of minimizing the risk. Finally, the measure is proportionate in terms of effects: the positive effects associated with the limit are significant, while the impact on the claimants, while not trivial, does not deprive them of the ability to follow their religious convictions.

DISSENT OF JUSTICE ABELLA

While Justice Abella, in a lengthy dissent, accepted the legitimacy of the photo identification goal, she did question the extent of its importance. She wrote:

> Alberta acknowledged that it is not attempting to justify the photo requirement on the basis that it allows for quick and efficient driver identification at the side of the road. The exemption to the photograph requirement was in place for 29 years without any demonstrably negative effects on roadside enforcement.
>
> Instead, Alberta stated that the purpose of the mandatory photo requirement was to ensure that every individual who has applied for a licence is represented in the Province's facial recognition database. This database helps prevent an individual from applying for a licence in another person's name. Driver's licences are a widely accepted form of identification. False licences can be used to gain other fraudulent documentation. The objective, therefore, is to protect the integrity of

the licensing system and its consequential benefit is the minimization of the risk of identity theft.

The majority rejects the Colony's alternative proposal of a photoless licence stamped with an indication that it not be used for identification purposes, on the grounds that "the only way to reduce that risk [of misusing driver's licences for identity theft] as much as possible is through a universal photo requirement" and "the alternative proposed by the claimants would significantly compromise the government's objective." ... But there is no cogent or persuasive evidence of any such dramatic interference with the government's objective....

The positive impact of the mandatory photo requirement and the use of facial recognition technology is that it is a way to help ensure that individuals will not be able to commit identity theft. But the facial recognition technology is hardly foolproof. Joseph Mark Pendleton, Director of the Special Investigations Unit of the Alberta Ministry of Government Services, acknowledged in his affidavit on behalf of the Government of Alberta, that "facial recognition software is not so advanced that it can make a definitive determination of whether two photographs are of the same person." The software merely narrows down potentially similar faces to a manageable number. A human investigator must still "eyeball" the pictures to determine if they are the same person.

There is, in fact, no evidence from the government to suggest that the Condition Code G licences, in place for 29 years as an exemption to the photo requirement, caused any harm at all to the integrity of the licensing system. As a result, there is no basis for determining why the exemption is no longer feasible, or so dramatically obstructs the government's objective that it cannot be re-instated....

700,000 Albertans are without a driver's licence. That means that 700,000 Albertans have no photograph in the system that can be checked by facial recognition technology. While adding approximately 250 licence holders to the database will reduce some opportunity for identity theft, it is hard to see how it will make a significant impact on preventing it when there are already several hundred thousand unlicenced and therefore unphotographed Albertans. Since there are so many others who are not in the database, the benefit of adding the photographs of the few Hutterites who wish to drive would be marginal.

It is worth noting too that in Alberta, numerous documents are used for identity purposes, including birth certificates, social insurance cards and health cards — not all of which include a photograph. Nor has Alberta thought it necessary to introduce, for example, a universal identity card to prevent identity theft. This suggests that the risk is not sufficiently compelling to justify universality.

The fact that Alberta is seemingly unengaged by the impact on identity theft of over 700,000 Albertans being without a driver's licence makes it difficult to understand why it feels that the system cannot tolerate 250 or so more exemptions.

The harm to the religious rights of the Hutterites weighs more heavily. The majority assesses the Wilson Colony members' freedom of religion as being a choice between having their picture taken or not having a driver's licence which may have collateral effects on their way of life. This, with respect, is not a meaningful choice for the Hutterites.

To suggest, as the majority does, that the deleterious effects are minor because the Colony members could simply arrange for third party transportation, fails to appreciate the significance of their self-sufficiency to the autonomous integrity of their religious community. When significant sacrifices have to be made to practise one's religion in the face of a state imposed burden, the choice to practise one's religion is no longer uncoerced.

The mandatory photo requirement is a form of indirect coercion that places the Wilson Colony members in the untenable position of having to choose between compliance with their religious beliefs or giving up the self-sufficiency of their community, a community that has historically preserved its religious autonomy through its communal independence.

The burden under section 1 is squarely on the government. That is where it should rigorously remain, without diminution for any reason. The majority's approach — making the right dependent on a formalistic distinction and characterization of the nature of the law — creates, even if inadvertently, a legal hierarchy attracting diminishing levels of scrutiny. This not only imperils and contradicts human rights jurisprudence, it risks presumptively shrinking the plenitude of what is captured by freedom of religion in s. 2(a) of the Charter by tethering its scope to an artificial stratum of government action. (See McLachlin C.J. "Freedom of Religion and the Rule of Law: A Canadian Perspective" in Douglas Farrow, ed.,

Recognizing Religion in a Secular Society: Essays in Pluralism, Religion, and Public Policy (2004), 12.)

The harm to the Hutterites' Charter right is substantial and easily ascertainable, but, as previously noted, the benefit of requiring the Hutterites to be photographed for the purposes of reducing identity theft, is not. Hundreds of thousands of Albertans have no driver's licence and their photographs, therefore, are not available in the facial recognition database, to help minimize identity theft. It is not clear to me how having approximately 250 additional Hutterites' photographs in the database will be of any significance in enhancing the government's objective, compared to the seriousness of the intrusion into the Hutterites' religious autonomy.

What we are left with is the desire to protect Albertans from the risks and costs associated with identity theft through a mandatory photo requirement, versus the cost to the Hutterites, religious and democratic, of not having their constitutional rights respected. Here, the constitutional right is significantly impaired; the "costs" to the public only slightly so, if at all.

Given the disproportion in this case between the harmful effects of the mandatory photo requirement on religious freedom, compared to the minimal salutary effects of requiring photographs from the Hutterites, the government has not discharged its burden of demonstrating that the infringement is justified under s. 1. This makes the mandatory photograph requirement for driver's licences, in the absence of the availability of an exemption on religious grounds, inconsistent with section 2(a) of the Charter.

I would therefore dismiss the appeal, but would suspend a declaration of invalidity for one year to give Alberta an opportunity to fashion a responsive amendment.

(*Globe and Mail*, July 27, 2009; *Globe and Mail*, August 15, 2009; *Globe and Mail*, August 21, 2009)

PRAYER SPACE FOR STUDENTS

The Muslim faith requires its followers to pray five times a day for five minutes, at intervals of roughly two to three hours. Students at two Quebec universities, unhappy with the lack of appropriate prayer spaces on campus, took action to remedy the situation.

In 2003 a $1.1 million complaint was filed on behalf of 113 Muslim students at Montreal's Ecole de technologie supérieure (ETS), the engineering school affiliated with the University of Quebec. Students had complained that they were forced to kneel on prayer carpets in crowded stairwells because the school, citing its in-house policy of excluding religious groups, was unwilling to provide a separate prayer room.

On March 22, 2006, the Quebec Human Rights Commission ruled that the school was obligated to "allow students of the Muslim faith to pray, on a regular basis, in conditions that respect their right to the safeguard of their dignity." ETS was given sixty days to remedy the problem. Marc-André Dowd, interim president of the commission, pointed out that other universities had created multi-faith or meditation rooms to meet the needs of their growing Muslim student bodies. Setting aside empty classrooms was suggested.

Five days later, ETS announced that it would provide Muslim students with a schedule of fifty-six classrooms available throughout the day to use as prayer space (*Globe and Mail*, March 23, 2006).

REFERENCES AND FURTHER READING
* Cited by the Supreme Court of Canada.

Bailey, Sue. "Hutterites Lose Court Case Over Photos." *Globe and Mail,* July 27, 2009.

Barak, Aharon. 2007. "Proportional Effect: The Israeli Experience." *University of Toronto Law Journal* 57: 369.*

Blackwell, Richard. "Kirpan Ban Overturned." *Globe and Mail,* March 3, 2006.

Cameron, Jamie. 1997. "The Past, Present, and Future of Expressive Freedom Under the *Charter*." *Osgoode Hall Law Journal* 35: 1.*

Choudhry, Sujit. 2006. "So What Is the Real Legacy of Oakes? Two Decades of Proportionality Analysis Under the Canadian Charter's Section 1." *Supreme Court Law Review* (2d series) 34: 501.*

Davis, Morris and Joseph F. Krauter. 1971. *The Other Canadians: Profiles of Six Minorities.* Toronto: Methuen.*

Eissen, Marc-André. 1993. "The Principle of Proportionality in the Case-Law of the European Court of Human Rights." In R. St. J. Macdonald, F. Matscher and H. Petzold, eds., *The European System for the Protection of Human Rights.* Dordrecht, The Netherlands: Martinus Nijhoff.*

Globe and Mail. "No Real Risk of Identity Theft." August 15, 2009.

Grimm, Dieter. 2007. "Proportionality in Canadian and German Constitutional Jurisprudence." *University of Toronto Law Journal* 57: 383.*

Makin, Kirk. "Top Court to Weigh School Ban on Kirpan." *Globe and Mail,* April 12, 2005.

McLachlin, Beverley M. (Chief Justice Supreme Court of Canada). 2004. "Freedom of Religion and the Rule of Law: A Canadian Perspective." In Douglas Farrow, ed., *Recognizing Religion in a Secular Society: Essays in Pluralism, Religion, and Public Policy.* Montreal and Kingston: McGill-Queen's University Press.*

Nussbaum, Martha. 2008. *Liberty of Conscience: In Defense of America's Tradition of Religious Equality*. New York: Basic Books.*

Pennings, Ray. "The Hutterite Driver's Licence Ruling Misses the Big Picture." *Globe and Mail*, August 21, 2009.

Peritz, Ingrid. "Find Prayer Space, School Told." *Globe and Mail*, March 23, 2006.

Taylor, Charles. 1995. *Philosophical Arguments*. Cambridge, MA: Harvard University Press.*

Webber, Jeremy. 2006. "The Irreducibly Religious Content of Freedom of Religion." In Avigail Eisenberg, ed., *Diversity and Equality: The Changing Framework of Freedom in Canada*. Vancouver: UBC Press.*

_____. 2008. "Understanding the Religion in Freedom of Religion." In Peter Cane, Carolyn Evans and Zoë Robinson, eds., *Law and Religion in Theoretical and Historical Context*. Cambridge, UK: Cambridge University Press.*

5

CHAPTER 5

INDECENCY DEFINED: THE QUESTION OF HARM

Section 2(b) of the Charter relates to freedom of expression. We will now focus on the kind of expression that the criminal law long has condemned: indecency.

Among the questions raised in this chapter are:

- Under the Criminal Code, does morality determine "acts of indecency"?
- Is a "community standard of tolerance" an objective standard?
- How is a "risk of harm to the community" proved?

What is "indecency" or "acts of indecency" under the Criminal Code? Under section 210(1) of the Criminal Code, the "practice of acts of indecency" is made an offence punishable by two years in prison. The offence, under this provision, relates to keeping a "common bawdy-house." This is defined as a place kept, occupied, or resorted to "by one or more persons for the purpose of prostitution or the practice of acts of indecency" (section 197(1) of the Criminal Code).

Parliament, however, did not define the "practice of acts of indecency." Without Parliamentary definition written into law, giving definition was left to the courts because, in the final analysis, the courts must pass upon the law in determining guilt or innocence. It is a task that Chief Justice McLachlin of the Supreme Court of Canada has called "notoriously difficult."

The difficulty is a result of judges having only past decisions rooted in the principle of community tolerance to guide them. In other words, how would the community, as a whole, tolerate other Canadians engaging in the questioned acts? This introduced a large measure of "subjectivity" or value judgment by each judge.

In *The Queen v. Labaye*, [2005] *Supreme Court Cases* 728, the Supreme Court of Canada re-examined the community tolerance test for determining indecency under section 210(1) of the Criminal Code. The Court, in a 7–2 decision, adopted a different test for deciding whether an act is indecent. Chief Justice McLachlin spoke for the Court majority. Justices Michel Bastarache and Louis LeBel dissented in an opinion written by Justice Bastarache.

THE QUEEN V. LABAYE: THE MAJORITY OPINION

Chief Justice McLachlin, in an opening statement for the Court majority in the Labaye case, gave the context for discussion. She wrote:

> Defining indecency under the Criminal Code is a notoriously difficult enterprise. The Criminal Code offers no assistance, leaving the task to judges. The test developed by the cases has evolved from one based largely on subjective considerations, to one emphasizing the need for objective criteria, based on harm.
>
> This heightened emphasis on objective criteria rests on the principle that crimes should be defined in a way that affords citizens, police and the courts a clear idea of what acts are prohibited.... We

generally convict and imprison people only where
it is established beyond a reasonable doubt that they
have violated objectively defined norms. Crimes
relating to public indecency are no exception.

On the facts and the law, the majority opinion in the Labaye
case differed sharply from the dissent of Justices Bastarache and
LeBel. We will set out the facts, as stated by the majority, and leave
it to the reader to compare those facts with the dissenting view.
We will do the same in relation to the majority view of the law.
Here, however, we will note the majority conclusions, arrived at
after analysis, that the status of the law was both ambiguous and
called upon judges to use much subjective judgment.

More important, in our view, is the fundamental decision of
the Supreme Court to change direction — to set a new test for
defining indecency under section 210(1) of the Criminal Code.
We will give the larger portion of this section over to the statement
and explanation of that test, as given by Chief Justice McLachlin,
speaking for a majority of the Court.

THE FACTS OF THE CASE

The accused operated a club in Montreal called l'Orage. The purpose
of the club was to permit couples and single people to meet each other
for group sex, and that meant explicit sex in certain designated and
ostensibly private areas of the club. Only members and their guests
were admitted to the club. Members paid an annual membership fee.

L'Orage had three floors. The first floor was occupied by a bar,
the second by a salon, and the third by what was called the "apartment" of the accused. A doorman controlled the main door of the
club, to ensure that only members and their guests entered. Two
doors separated access to the third floor apartment from the rest
of the club. One was marked "Privé" ("Private") and the other was
locked with a numeric key pad.

Members of the club were supplied with the appropriate code and permitted to access the third floor apartment. This was the only place where group sex took place. A number of mattresses were scattered about the floor of the apartment. There, people engaged in a variety of sexual acts. There was participation by members in some of the acts, and also observation by members.

Entry to the club and participation in the activities were voluntary. No one was forced to do anything or watch anything. No one was paid for sex. While men considerably outnumbered women on the occasions when the police visited, there was no suggestion that any of the women were there involuntarily or that they did not willingly engage in the acts of group sex.

Thus, among the important findings, as stated by Chief Justice McLachlin, were:

1. The questioned sexual activities were *private*. They were not open to the public.
2. Those who participated in these activities, either actively or as spectators, did so *voluntarily*.
3. No money, as such, was paid for this member participation.

The trial court, following hearings, ruled that the accused was guilty of indecency within the meaning of section 210(1) of the Criminal Code. The judge stated that, in fact, the acts occurred in a public place, as defined by the Criminal Code, because *the public had a right of access, either by membership or invitation*. And, she said, the sexual practices fell below the Canadian community standard of tolerance. The conduct of those participating, she ruled, was calculated to induce anti-social behaviour in disregard of moral values, and such conduct raised the risk of sexually transmitted disease.

A majority of the Quebec Court of Appeal upheld the conviction. In the view of the court majority, the voluntary character of member and guest participation did not diminish the "resulting degradation, loss of integrity and self-respect."

However, Justice Michel Proulx dissented, arguing:

> Even if the establishment was a public place, as
> defined in the Criminal Code, members of the
> club did not perform the sexual acts in open public
> view, but in a context of relative privacy. Entrants
> were screened and informed. All the participants
> retained their full autonomy. The sexual exchanges
> they participated in reflected their personal choice
> and view of sexuality. Since there was no meaning-
> ful distinction between participants and observ-
> ers, the presence of observers was not relevant
> for assessing the publicly indecent character of
> the activities. Moreover, there was no social harm
> comparable to ... where the payment of women for
> sexual services led to an inference of exploitation.

The Supreme Court allowed the appeal and, in a 7–2 decision,
it set aside the conviction.

THE STATUS OF THE LAW: A SEARCH FOR OBJECTIVITY

In the Labaye case, the chief justice spoke of a movement away
from the personal judgment of a court as to whether an act was
indecent under the criminal law. That movement was toward a
more *objective standard.*

At its start, under English common law — that is, law as
stated by the courts and followed by them as precedent —- the
standard for obscenity was whether material would tend to
deprave and corrupt other members of society. But, Chief Justice
McLachlin said: "Depravity and corruption vary with the eye of
the beholder, and the [early English] test proved difficult to apply
in an objective fashion. Convictions often depended more on
the idiosyncrasies and the subjective moral views of the judge or

jurors than objective criteria of what might deprave or corrupt. Nevertheless, the [English] test remained in place for almost a century."

In 1959 the Canadian Parliament introduced a new "undue exploitation of sex" test for obscene materials, now section 163(8) of the Criminal Code. In considering this test, the Supreme Court emphasized the failings of the previous test and the need for new criteria "which have some certainty of meaning and are capable of objective application and which do not so much depend as before upon the idiosyncrasies and sensitivities of the tribunal of fact, whether judge or jury" (*Brodie v. The Queen*, [1962] *Supreme Court of Canada Reports* 681).

However, said Chief Justice McLachlin, the goal of objectivity was not reached. She stated:

> Borrowing on decisions from Australia and New Zealand emphasizing the foundation of criminal legislation on obscenity and indecency in societal norms, the Court adopted a test based on the community standard of tolerance. On its face, the test was objective, requiring the trier of fact to determine what the community would tolerate.
>
> Yet once again, in practice it proved difficult to apply in an objective fashion. How does one determine what the "community" would tolerate were it aware of the conduct or material? In a diverse, pluralistic society whose members hold divergent views, who is the "community"? And how can one objectively determine what the community, if one could define it, would tolerate, in the absence of evidence that community knew of and considered the conduct in question?
>
> In practice, once again, the test tended to function as a proxy [means] for the personal

views of expert witnesses, judges and jurors. In the end, the question often came down to what they, as individual members of the community, would tolerate. Judges and jurors were unlikely, human nature being what it is, to see themselves and their beliefs as intolerant. It was far more likely that they would see themselves as reasonable, representative members of the community. The chances of a judge or juror saying "I view this conduct as indecent but I set that view aside because it is intolerant" were remote indeed. The result was that despite its superficial objectivity, the community standard of tolerance test remained highly subjective in application.

In 1985 the Supreme Court continued the search for objectivity by introducing a two-part definition of community standards of tolerance in *Towne Cinema Theatres Ltd. v. The Queen*, [1985] 1 *Supreme Court Reports* 494. The first way to establish obscenity (undue exploitation of sex) was to show that the material violated the norm of tolerance of what Canadians would permit others, whose views they did not share, to do or see. The second was to show that the material would have a harmful effect on others in society. The Towne Cinema case marked the first clear statement of the relationship between obscenity and harm in Canadian law, and represented the *beginning of a shift from a community standards test to a harm-based test.*

The shift to a harm-based basis of reasoning was completed by the Supreme Court's decisions in *The Queen v. Butler*, [1992] 1 *Supreme Court of Canada Reports* 452, and *Little Sisters Book and Art Emporium v. Canada (Minister of Justice)*, [2000] 2 *Supreme Court of Canada Reports* 1120. In the Butler case, the two-part test for obscenity of the Towne Cinema case was fused into a single test in which the community standard of tolerance was determined by reference to the risk of harm flowing from the questioned conduct.

The Court in the Little Sisters case confirmed that harm is an essential ingredient of obscenity. As Justice Binnie stated: "The phrase 'degrading and dehumanizing' in *Butler* is qualified immediately by the words 'if the risk of harm is substantial.' This makes it clear that not all sexually explicit erotica depicting adults engaged in conduct which is considered to be degrading or dehumanizing is obscene. The material must also create a substantial risk of harm which exceeds the community's tolerance."

Chief Justice McLachlin said that the Labaye case allowed the Supreme Court to provide "further definition" of the "harm" principle. She wrote:

> Grounding criminal indecency in harm represents an important advance in this difficult area of the law. Harm or significant risk of harm is easier to prove than a community standard. Moreover, the requirement of a risk of harm incompatible with the proper functioning of society brings this area of the law into step with the vast majority of criminal offences, which are based on the need to protect society from harm.
>
> However, it is not always clear precisely how the harm test for indecency applies in particular circumstances. New cases have raised questions as to the nature and degree of harm sufficient to establish indecency. Further definition is required in order to resolve cases like this, and to permit individuals to conduct themselves within the law and the police and courts to enforce the criminal sanction in an objective, fair way.

THE HARM TEST

The chief justice set out two general requirements necessary for a finding of indecency:

1. The harm must be of the kind "recognized in [the Canadian constitution] or similar fundamental laws." Put somewhat differently, the opposite side of "harm" relates to values that the Constitution or other fundamental laws are designed to protect.

   An expression of such values can be found in the Canadian Charter of Rights and Freedoms, which is part of the Constitution of Canada. For example, section 7 of the Charter provides that "everyone has the right to life, liberty and security of the person and the right not to be deprived thereof except in accordance with the principles of fundamental justice." This is, in part, a constitutional expression going to the dignity of the individual. Similarly, human rights codes, both at the federal and provincial levels, tend to re-enforce such rights by prohibiting discrimination on the bases of race, religion, gender, and disability — among other grounds.

   The chief justice suggested that the rights and values noted are those "formally recognized" by Canadian law. As such, the criminal law, such as those relating to indecency, might directly enforce those rights and values.

   But, this is only the first step. It is concerned with the *nature of the harm*. The chief justice said: "The first step asks whether the Crown has established a harm or significant risk of harm to others that is grounded in norms which our society has formally recognized in its Constitution or similar fundamental laws."

2. We come now to the second step in the Court's more detailed definition going to *objectivity*. This step is concerned with the *degree of harm*. In the words of Chief Justice McLachlin:

"It asks whether the harm in its degree is incompatible with the proper functioning of society."

In the Labaye case, the Court went to some length to provide detail for both elements. In doing so it noted that each element must be proved beyond reasonable doubt before an act can be considered indecent under the Criminal Code.

THE NATURE OF HARM

The Court dealt first with the nature of harm. The chief justice stated:

> Three types of harm have thus far emerged from the jurisprudence as being capable of supporting a finding of indecency: (1) harm to those whose autonomy and liberty may be restricted by being confronted with inappropriate conduct; (2) harm to society by predisposing others to anti-social conduct; and (3) harm to individuals participating in the conduct.
>
> Each of these types of harm is grounded in values recognized by our Constitution and similar fundamental laws. The list is not closed; other types of harm may be shown in the future to meet the standards for criminality established.... But thus far, these are the types of harm recognized by the cases.

The second source of harm, said the chief justice, is the kind that "predisposes others to anti-social acts or attitudes, such as the physical or mental mistreatment of women by men or, less likely, the reverse. She wrote:

> This source of harm is not confined to explicit invitations or exhortations to commit anti-social

acts.... The inquiry embraces attitudinal harm. Conduct or material that perpetuates negative and demeaning images of humanity is likely to undermine respect for members of the targeted groups and hence to predispose others to act in an anti-social manner towards them. Such conduct may violate formally recognized societal norms, like the equality and dignity of all human beings, which is protected by the Canadian Charter of Rights and Freedoms and similar fundamental laws such as the provincial human rights codes.

Because this source of harm involves members of the public being exposed to the conduct or material, here, too [as in the first type of harm], it is relevant to inquire whether the conduct is private or public. This type of harm can arise only if members of the public may be exposed to the conduct or material in question.

A third source of harm, physical and/or psychological, is that affecting participating individuals. The chief justice stated:

Sexual activity is a positive source of human expression, fulfilment and pleasure. But some kinds of sexual activity may harm those involved. Women may be forced into prostitution or other aspects of the sex trade. They may be the objects of physical and psychological assault. Sometimes they may be seriously hurt or even killed. Similar harms may be perpetrated on children and men. Sexual conduct that risks this sort of harm may violate society's declared norms in a way that is incompatible with the proper functioning of society, and hence meet the ... test for indecent conduct under the Criminal Code.

The consent of the participant will generally be significant in considering whether this type of harm is established. However, consent may be more apparent than real. Courts must always be on the lookout for the reality of victimization. Where other aspects of debased treatment are clear, harm to participating individuals may be established despite apparent consent.

Unlike the previous types of harm by confrontation and by inculcation [instruction], the third type of harm is only minimally dependent on whether the conduct is private or public, since its focus is not on harm to society or members of society, but on individuals involved in the acts. Harm of this type is not dependent on public viewing, and may occur in a private room of an establishment, so long as the minimal element of publicity is satisfied to bring it within the scope of the indecency provisions, by showing it to be a place kept for the purpose of practising such acts, for instance. *In the final analysis, the critical issue is not how members of the public might be affected, but how the participant is affected* [emphasis added].

THE DEGREE OF HARM

We come now to the degree of harm. The harm, we will assume, fits under one of the three classes set out by Chief Justice McLachlin. For there to be a finding of indecency, there must be the necessary extent or degree of harm. Chief Justice McLachlin stated:

At this stage, the task is to examine the degree of the harm to determine whether it is incompatible with the proper functioning of society. The threshold is high. It proclaims that as members of a diverse society, we must be prepared to tolerate conduct of which we disapprove, short of conduct that can be objectively shown beyond a reasonable doubt to interfere with the proper functioning of society.

Only if the impact of the acts in degree of harm poses a real risk of damaging the autonomy and liberty of members of the public, judged by contemporary standards, can indecency be established.

Incompatibility with the proper functioning of society is more than a test of tolerance. The question is not what individuals or the community think about the conduct, but whether permitting it engages a harm that threatens the basic functioning of our society. This ensures in part that the harm be related to a formally recognized value, at step one. But beyond this it must be clear beyond a reasonable doubt that the conduct, not only by its nature but also in degree, rises to the level of threatening the proper functioning of our society.

Whether it does so must be determined by reference to the values engaged by the particular kind of harm at stake. If the harm is based on the threat to autonomy and liberty arising from unwanted confrontation by a particular kind of sexual conduct, for example, the Crown must establish a real risk that the way people live will be significantly and adversely affected by the conduct. The number of people unwillingly exposed to the conduct and the circumstances in which they are exposed to it are critical under this head of harm. If the only people involved in or observing the conduct were willing participants, indecency on the basis of this harm will not be made out.

If the harm is based on predisposing others to anti-social behaviour, a real risk that the conduct will have this effect must be proved. Vague generalizations that the sexual conduct at issue will lead to attitudinal changes and hence anti-social behaviour will not suffice. The causal link between images of sexuality and anti-social behaviour cannot be assumed. Attitudes in themselves are not crimes, however deviant they may be or disgusting they may appear. What is required is proof of links, first between the sexual conduct at issue and the formation of negative attitudes, and second between those attitudes and real risk of anti-social behaviour.

Similarly, if the harm is based on physical or psychological injury to participants, it must again be shown that the harm has occurred or that there is a real risk that this will occur. Witnesses may testify as to actual harm. Expert witnesses may give evidence on the risks of potential harm. In considering psychological harm, care must be taken to avoid substituting disgust for the conduct involved, for proof of harm to the participants. In the case of vulnerable participants, it may be easier to infer psychological harm than in cases where participants operate on an equal and autonomous basis.

These are matters that can and should be established by evidence, as a general rule. When the test was the community standard of tolerance, it could be argued that judges or jurors were in a position to gauge what the community would tolerate from their own experience in the community. But a test of harm or significant risk of harm incompatible with the proper functioning of society demands more. The judge and jurors are generally unlikely to be able to gauge the risk and impact of the harm, without assistance from expert witnesses. To be sure, there may be obvious cases where no one could argue that the conduct proved in evidence is compatible with the proper functioning of society, obviating the need for an expert witness.

To kill in the course of sexual conduct, to take an obvious example, would on its face be repugnant to our law and the proper functioning of our society. But in most cases, expert evidence will be required to establish that the nature and degree of the harm makes it incompatible with the proper functioning of society. In every case, a conviction must be based on evidence establishing beyond a reasonable doubt actual harm or a significant risk of actual harm. The focus on evidence helps to render the inquiry more objective. It does not, however, transform the entire inquiry into a pure question of fact. A finding of indecency requires the application of a legal standard to the facts and context surrounding the impugned conduct. It is this legal standard that the harm-based test seeks to articulate.

Where actual harm is not established and the Crown is relying on risk, the test of incompatibility with the proper functioning of society requires the Crown to establish a significant risk. Risk is a relative concept. The more extreme the nature of the harm, the lower the degree of risk that may be required to permit use of the ultimate sanction of criminal law. Sometimes, a small risk can be said to be incompatible with the proper functioning of society. For example, the risk of a terrorist attack, although small, might be so devastating in potential impact that using the criminal law to counter the risk might be appropriate. However, in most cases, the nature of the harm engendered by sexual conduct will require at least a probability that the risk will develop to justify convicting and imprisoning those engaged in or facilitating the conduct.

APPLYING THE TEST

The Court majority in *The Queen v. Labaye* reviewed the three types of harm spelled out in the "test." It found, on the facts, that none of the three types of harm occurred. We will state the Court's findings in detail:

> The sexual acts at issue were conducted on the third floor of a private club, behind doors marked "Privé" and accessed only by persons in possession of the proper numerical code. The evidence establishes that a number of steps were taken to ensure that members of the public who might find the conduct inappropriate did not see the activities. Pre-membership interviews were conducted to advise of the nature of the activities and screen out persons not sharing the same interests. Only members and guests were admitted to the premises. A doorman controlled access to the principal door.
>
> On these facts, none of the kinds of harm discussed above was established. The autonomy and liberty of members of the public was not affected by unwanted confrontation with the sexual

conduct in question. On the evidence, only those already disposed to this sort of sexual activity were allowed to participate and watch.

Nor was there evidence of the second type of harm, the harm of predisposing people to anti-social acts or attitudes. Unlike the material at issue in *Butler*, which perpetuated abusive and humiliating stereotypes of women as objects of sexual gratification, there is no evidence of anti-social attitudes toward women, or for that matter men. No one was pressured to have sex, paid for sex, or treated as a mere sexual object for the gratification of others. The fact that l'Orage is a commercial establishment does not in itself render the sexual activities taking place there commercial in nature. Members do not pay a fee and check consent at the door; the membership fee buys access to a club where members can meet and engage in consensual activities with other individuals who have similar sexual interests. The case proceeded on the uncontested premise that all participation was on a voluntary and equal basis.

Finally, there is no evidence of the third type of harm — physical or psychological harm to persons participating. The only possible danger to participants on the evidence was the risk of catching a sexually transmitted disease. However, this must be discounted as a factor because, as discussed above, it is conceptually and causally unrelated to indecency.

As stated above, the categories of harm are not closed; in a future case other different harms may be alleged as a basis for criminal indecency. However, no other harms are raised by the evidence in this case. All that is raised, in the final analysis, is the assessment that the conduct amounted to "an orgy" and that Canadian society does not tolerate orgies.... This reasoning erroneously harks back to the community standard of tolerance test, which has been replaced, as discussed, by the harm-based test....

I conclude that the evidence provides no basis for concluding that the sexual conduct at issue harmed individuals or society. Criminal indecency or obscenity must rest on actual harm or a significant risk of harm to individuals or society. The Crown failed to establish this essential element of the offence. The Crown's case must therefore fail. The majority of the Court of Appeal erred, with respect, in applying an essentially subjective community standard of tolerance test and failing to apply the harm-based test.

The Court saw no need to examine the second part of the harm-based test, namely the question going to the degree of harm.

SUMMARY OF THE TEST UNDER THE QUEEN V. LABAYE

Indecent criminal conduct will be established where the Crown proves beyond a reasonable doubt the following two requirements:

1. By its nature, the conduct challenged causes harm or presents a significant risk of harm to individuals or society in a way that undermines or threatens to undermine a value in the Constitution or similar fundamental laws by, for example:

(a) confronting members of the public with conduct that significantly interferes with their autonomy and liberty; or

(b) predisposing others to anti-social behaviour; or

(c) physically or psychologically harming persons involved in the conduct.

2. That the harm or risk of harm is of a degree that conflicts with the proper functioning of society.

The categories of harm in the first requirement are not closed, nor is any one of the listed categories in itself a necessary part of the definition of harm. For example, predisposition to anti-social behaviour is only one illustration of the type of harm that undermines or threatens to undermine one of society's formally recognized values.

This test, applied objectively and on the basis of evidence in successive cases as they arise, is directed to stating legal standards that, as Chief Justice Mclachlin wrote: "enhance the ability of persons engaged in or facilitating sexual activities to [know] the boundary between non-criminal conduct and criminal conduct. In this way, the basic requirements of the criminal law of fair notice to potential offenders and clear enforcement standards to police will, it is hoped, be satisfied."

DEFINITION — MORALITY OR LAW?

Question: Are "acts of indecency" defined by morality or law in terms of interpreting the Criminal Code?

Answer: The Court majority in the Labaye case made it clear that courts are to look to the law in giving meaning to "acts of indecency," though this was not to deny a relationship between the two. Chief Justice McLachlin, for the Court, stated:

> Indecency has two meanings, one moral and one legal. Our concern is not with the moral

aspect of indecency, but with the legal. The moral and legal aspects of the concept are, of course, related. Historically, the legal concepts of indecency and obscenity, as applied to conduct and publications, respectively, have been inspired and informed by the moral views of the community.

But over time, courts increasingly came to recognize that morals and taste were subjective, arbitrary and unworkable in the criminal context, and that a diverse society could function only with a generous measure of tolerance for minority mores and practices. This led to a legal norm of objectively ascertainable harm instead of subjective disapproval.

ANOTHER VIEW: THE DISSENT

As noted, Justices Bastarache and LeBel dissented in the Labaye case. Justice Bastarache, writing for the dissent, argued that social or public morality of the entire Canadian community does have a direct role to play in determining whether an act is indecent within the meaning of the Criminal Code. *It impacts directly on defining the applicable standard of tolerance.* He wrote:

Nonetheless, where indecency is concerned, place and context are relevant to the establishment of the applicable limits when assessing certain sexual acts and their conformity to the standards of tolerance of the Canadian community. By reason of the nature of the standard of tolerance, applying it necessarily entails a choice of values that relate to social or public morality and are recognized by the entire Canadian community as minimum, but mandatory, standards.

The standard of tolerance does not impose a morality based on particular religious beliefs or particular ideologies. It implements a social morality that is the product of values characteristic of the entire community. These values generally reflect a social consensus that manifests itself through, for example, a concern for ... the dignity of individuals and their autonomy, potential for development and fundamental equality.

What must be done is not, therefore, to choose the preferences of a particular social group and impose them on others. Rather, it is necessary to establish the degree of tolerance of the majority of the Canadian community as a whole toward sexual acts, taking their context, including the place where they occur, into account. The test for indecency thus remains sufficiently objective, because it is based on a social consensus among Canadians as to what is acceptable in terms of sexual practices."

YOU BE THE JUDGE

PUBLIC VIEW: OBSCENITY?

The case that follows was suggested in *The Queen v. Labaye.*

THE FACTS

Bert Johnson owns a bar near a solid "blue collar" residential neighbourhood. Business has been slow but he believes that he has a way to increase profits. He will advertise the bar as one where adults may take off their clothes, and they may touch one another — assuming consent has been given. Force and intimidation will be expressly forbidden, and these rules will be fully enforced.

But, what will make his bar "unique," in Johnson's view, is that a wide-screen video will display — without sound — what takes place in the bar. Johnson will advertise: "Here's your chance to be outlandish." In fact, to test public interest, Johnson has gone ahead with the wide-screen video, and some of the scenes shown involve nudity and fondling among patrons. The videos are projected in a large window of the bar for passersby to see.

There are a number of houses of worship close to Johnson's bar. All the neighbourhood ministers and clerics (numbering about twenty), strongly urged on by their parishioners, want an end to the public display of the bar's wide-screen video.

The police and Crown have been quick to respond. Charges have been laid against Johnson and his business, directed specifically at the wide-screen public display video. Those charges have been brought under section 163(8) of the Criminal Code which provides: "For the purposes of this Act, any publication a dominant characteristic of which is the undue exploitation of sex, or of sex and any one or more of the following subjects, namely, crime, horror, cruelty and violence, shall be deemed to be obscene."

THE ISSUE

Is the public display of the wide-screen videos of nudity and sexual fondling taking place inside the bar obscene within the meaning of section 163(8) of the Criminal Code in that it is an "undue exploitation of sex"?

POINTS TO CONSIDER

- For purposes of the Criminal Code, obscenity and indecency are treated as having the same meaning.
- In a well-structured survey, the view of the ministers and clerics was found accurately to reflect that of their colleagues nationally.
- The same survey found that, if the community is defined as the neighbourhood around Johnson's bar or even the city where it is located, an overwhelming number of residents find the publicly displayed videos obscene.
- The "values" that laws against obscenity or indecency are intended to uphold, according to the decision in the Labaye case, are fundamental to Canadian society as a whole.
- Such "fundamental" values include: autonomy, liberty, equality, and human dignity.

DISCUSSION

The chief justice, speaking for the Court majority in *The Queen v. Labaye,* suggested that the law against obscenity in the kind of fact situation presented would not be allowed. This was the first of three types of harm such laws are designed to prohibit: "harm to those whose autonomy and liberty may be restricted by being confronted with inappropriate conduct." Those who walked by Johnson's bar or lived in the neighbourhood have important rights, even fundamental rights, the chief justice seemed to say. An invasion of these rights would reduce their "quality of life."

The chief justice stated:

> First is the harm of public confrontation with unacceptable and inappropriate conduct. One reason for criminalizing indecent acts and displays is to protect the public from being confronted with acts and material that reduce their quality of life. Indecent acts are banned because they subject the public to unwanted confrontation with inappropriate conduct.
>
> This harm is conceptually akin to nuisance. Nevertheless, to call this eyesore the basis of criminalization of indecent acts is to trivialize the harm. The harm is not the aesthetic harm of a less attractive community, but the loss of autonomy and liberty that public indecency may impose on individuals in society, as they seek to avoid confrontation with acts they find offensive and

unacceptable. The value or interest protected is the autonomy and liberty of members of the public, to live within a zone that is free from conduct that deeply offends them.

We live in an age when sexual images, some subtle and some not so subtle, are widely dispersed throughout our public space. However, this does not negate the fact that even in our emancipated society, there may be some kinds of sexual conduct the public display of which seriously impairs the livability of the environment and significantly constrains autonomy. Sexual relations are an intensely personal, religious and age-sensitive matter.

People's autonomy and enjoyment of life can be deeply affected by being unavoidably confronted with debased public sexual displays. Even when avoidance is possible, the result may be diminished freedom to go where they wish or take their children where they want. Sexual conduct and material that presents a risk of seriously curtailing people's autonomy and liberty may justifiably be restricted. The loss of autonomy and liberty to ordinary people by in-your-face indecency is a potential harm to which the law is entitled to respond. If the risk of harm is significant enough, it may rise to the degree of the test for criminal indecency — conduct which society formally recognizes as incompatible with its proper functioning.

Since the harm in this class of case is based on the public being confronted with unpalatable acts or material, it is essential that there be a risk that members of the public either will be unwillingly exposed to the conduct or material, or that they will be forced to significantly change their usual conduct to avoid being so exposed.

RELIGIOUS VIEWS AND OBSCENITY

Yet, how are the values of Canadian society to be determined? What is to be said of views of the ministers and the clerics? Don't their conclusions, supported by their members, go to define the values to be protected?

In this regard, the key words for the Supreme Court are *what values Canadian society has formally recognized.* Among other sources for that formal recognition by Canadian society is the Charter of Rights and Freedoms, part of the Constitution of Canada and, as such, the supreme law of the land.

This is what the chief justice had to say about religious freedom in the context of the law against obscenity:

The complexity of the guarantee of freedom of religion in this context requires further comment. The claim that particular sexual conduct violates particular religious rules or values does not alone suffice to establish this element of the test [for a finding of obscenity].

The question is what values Canadian society has formally recognized. Canadian society through its Constitution and similar fundamental laws does not formally recognize particular religious views, but rather the freedom to hold particular religious views. This freedom does not endorse any particular religious view, but the right to hold a variety of diverse views.

The requirement of formal endorsement ensures that people will not be convicted and imprisoned for transgressing the rules and beliefs of particular individuals or groups. To incur the ultimate criminal sanction, they must have violated values which Canadian society as a whole has formally endorsed.

CHALLENGE QUESTION

A MATTER OF OBJECTIVITY?

In the Labaye case, the Supreme Court, as noted, set a two-part harm-based test for determining indecency under section 210(1) of the Criminal Code. This was a change from a *community tolerance test* that had previously guided the Court in deciding such cases. In large part, the Court majority was motivated to make the change by the goal of *objectivity*. That is, criminal law, especially because it imposes penal sanctions (in the case of section 210(1) of up to two years in prison), ought to be clear so that the citizenry can understand what is expected of them, and police and courts can administer the law fairly.

Q. Does the new two-part test set out in The Queen v. Labaye eliminate subjective judgment on the part of judges?

The Court stated that the two-part harm-based test was more objective than the community tolerance test. But, the majority conceded that the new test left room for "value" judgment — especially in deciding whether the harm involved was incompatible with the proper functioning of Canadian society. But, the majority insisted that such "value" judgment need not be subjective.

The chief justice, speaking for the Court majority, stated:

> The objective test for criminal indecency that this Court has long insisted must be our goal requires careful and express analysis of whether the alleged harm is on the evidence in the particular case truly incompatible with the proper functioning of Canadian society. This involves value judgements. What is the "proper" functioning of society? At what point do we say an activity is "incompatible" with it?
>
> Value judgements in this domain of the law, like many others, cannot be avoided. But this does not mean that the decision-making process is subjective and arbitrary. First, judges should approach the task of making value judgments with an awareness of the danger of deciding the case on the basis of unarticulated and unacknowledged values or prejudices. Second, they should make value judgments on the

basis of evidence and a full appreciation of the relevant factual and legal context, to ensure that it is informed not by the judge's subjective views, but by relevant, objectively tested criteria. Third, they should carefully weigh and articulate the factors that produce the value judgements. By practices such as these, objectivity can be attained.

THE DISSENT

The dissent of Justices Bastarache and LeBel noted an element of subjectivity in the majority test. But, Justice Bastarache said, the community tolerance test does have within it the elements calling for objective judgment. In part, this arises from the reality that any such decision is treated as one of law and, as such, may be reviewed by a court as to its correctness. (Trial decisions of fact are generally given the presumption of correctness by a reviewing court.) Justice Bastarache stated:

In support of using harm as the basic test for establishing indecency, the majority cites the need to make the analysis more objective. It must be acknowledged, however, that a certain degree of subjectivity is inherent in the establishment of the standard of tolerance because of the judge's role as interpreter of the community's minimum standards regarding sex.

Despite this problem, the analysis remains objective on the whole as long as the judge ignores his or her personal convictions and instead tries to determine the nature of the social consensus. Judges must not only identify the harm addressed by the Criminal Code's provisions on indecency, but also determine the nature and content of the moral values of the community in which they perform their functions in order to establish the standard of tolerance.

The judge's role is not to review the evidence for the sole purpose of determining whether or not a particular social harm has been sustained and establishing the degree of that harm. His or her role is to resolve a question of law by assessing the nature of the acts in their context and evaluating them in relation to the practices and attitudes of Canadians. It is a difficult task, but [quoting Justice LeBel] "because it is a product of his or her times, shaped by his or her culture and concerns, the judge must assume the risks of the problems involved in identifying and reconciling values that are, at times, contradictory."

Despite the difficulties, the original test for tolerance should not be set aside to make way for a new one based solely on harm. The test was from the start designed to be a sufficiently objective standard, both conceptually and when applied to the facts.... Judges inquire into the behaviour and attitudes of Canadians relating to morals and then consider the parties' evidence on this issue. A choice of values is made, but the judge must subordinate his or her personal views on morality to community-wide standards. This approach makes it possible to uphold the values on which there is a social consensus and thereby ensure a sufficient level of objectivity. Following it does not appear to pose insurmountable problems for the courts.... Nor is this the only area in which judges must engage in such an exercise.

A TEST FULLY DEFINED?

Question: Is the harm-based test set out by the Supreme Court in *The Queen v. Labaye* a full statement of what now is required to prove indecency within the meaning of section 210(1) of the Criminal Code?
Answer: No. The chief justice in the Labaye case emphasized that this case arose as one calling for interpretation of a statute by the Court. While the Court made reference to "fundamental law," such as values contained in the Charter of Rights and Freedoms, which is part of the Constitution of Canada, the nature of the case required that it be treated "in the tradition of the common law." And this means that the law will be developed in the context of new cases as they arise.

The chief justice stated, for the Court majority: "Developing a workable theory of harm is not a task for a single case. In the tradition of the common law, its full articulation will come only as judges consider diverse situations and render decisions on them. Moreover, the difficulty of the task should not be underestimated. We must proceed incrementally, step by cautious step."

A STRONG AND LENGTHY DISSENT

Justices Bastarache and LeBel, as noted, issued a strong and lengthy dissent in *The Queen v. Labaye*. They saw no reason for ending the *community standard of tolerance test* to determine indecency under section 210(1) of the Criminal Code. They would have dismissed the appeal and upheld the conviction.

For the dissent, the standard of assessing the questioned act in the context of community tolerance allowed a judge to consider all the relevant factors as to whether an act was indecent. They acknowledged that among these factors could be (and often was) the element of harm. But, they emphasized that it was only one of the factors. And sometimes, they said, an act may be indecent even without the element of harm.

Justice Bastarache, who wrote the dissent, stated:

> There can be no doubt that ... social harm has [become] a very important test for establishing indecency.... However, despite the importance of the social harm test, it cannot be said to be the only standard by which the tolerance of the Canadian community for sexual practices is to be measured.
>
> The very definition of social harm warrants closer examination before this test can be applied to determine the level of tolerance of the Canadian community.... Bearing in mind the reasons that led to the adoption of the social harm test, it does not follow from [past cases] that the courts must determine what the community tolerates by reference to the degree of harm alone, and in particular of harm as it is defined by our colleagues in the majority in *Labaye*. The standard of tolerance is established by means of a contextual analysis....

Thus, serious harm is not the sole criterion for determining what the Canadian community will tolerate. Harm is but one indicator of the community standard of tolerance. The cases cited by the majority must be placed in the context of a line of authority that focusses on determining whether the standard of tolerance has been violated, based on the nature of the acts, the places where the acts occurred and the context. In our opinion, therefore, the majority's analysis departs in practice from the case law by adopting an approach based solely on harm.

CRITIQUE: THE ROLE OF THE JUDGE UNDER THE HARM TEST

Under the majority opinion in the Labaye case, *the role of the judge has changed.* According to Justice LeBel, past decisions, in effect, allowed reviewing courts a broader range in passing upon lower courts decisions as to whether an act was indecent under the Criminal Code. An explanation may be useful.

Not every decision of a trial court may be reviewed by an appellate court. Often the scope of such review is limited by whether the lower court decision is one of *fact* or *law*. If the decision of the lower court is found to be one of fact, then generally the appellate court is limited in its reviewing to the question as to whether there was sufficient evidence in the record (the proceedings before the trial court) to support the initial decision. There is a presumption of validity that usually accompanies a trial court's findings. *In effect, an appellate court has only a limited power to review the trial court's findings if they are limited to the facts only.*

On the other hand, if acts of indecency under the Criminal Code are deemed to be questions of law, appellate courts have a much broader scope for review of a trial court's decision. Appellate courts are not bound to give any presumptive validity to the decisions of a trial court. The appellate court can ask itself whether the lower court decision was, in the higher court's view, correct.

Justice LeBel seemed to argue that the majority decision in the Labaye case cut back the appellate court's range for review of what a trial court might decide. *It made such issues those of fact that are to be tested under a new broad standard of community harm rather than tolerance.*

This is how Justice LeBel put the matter:

> It is clear from the case law that the judge's role is, through contextual analysis, to interpret the community's view of sexual practices as expressed in various places at various times. Whether the impugned acts met the Canadian community standard of tolerance is thus a question of law.... *However, by adopting certain categories of harm that emphasize the mere exposure of the general public to sexual acts or the risk of serious psychological or physical harm, the majority's approach tends to reduce the judge's analysis to a purely fact-based one. The inquiry into the standard of tolerance thus becomes more a question of fact, which is contrary to this Court's case law* [emphasis added].

THE DISSENT: MEANING TO A "CONTEXTUAL APPROACH"

In the dissent of Justice Bastarache, the only way the standard of tolerance could be gauged is by placing the questioned act in context. Here, no one factor would be determinative. Rather, the reviewing court, as a matter of law, would inquire as to all the relevant factors.

To limit a court to harm for the purpose of section 210(1), said Justice Bastarache, would heavily impact practices or acts which Canadian society has long considered indecent. He offered as examples: child pornography, incest, polygamy, and bestiality. He stated:

> The community considers these acts to be harmful in themselves. Parliament enforces this social morality by enacting statutory norms in legislation such as the Criminal Code. The community does not tolerate degrading acts or sexual exploitation either.... Nor is the purchase of sexual favours in public places accepted, as evidenced by the various provisions of the Criminal Code that prohibit common bawdy-houses and prostitution.

> In this second type of situation, morality is conveyed by means of provisions that demand that each individual case be assessed in light of its specific context and circumstances in order to gauge the Canadian community's tolerance for the acts in question. Certain acts are thus prohibited because of their harmful nature. Others are prohibited because of the context and places in which they arise, as in [this case]. Harm is thus ultimately linked to a concept of social morality. There is also harm where what is acceptable to the community in terms of public morals is compromised.

> Thus, the need to prove societal [harm] to a degree approaching social disorder would appear to unduly restrict the situations in which a court could reach a finding of indecency. The importance of this requirement profoundly alters the traditional concept of tolerance by suggesting that the public will tolerate anything that is contrary

to public morals unless it can be established that an act will cause significant social disorder.

PUBLIC OR PRIVATE: ITS PLACE IN ANALYSIS

For the dissent, whether the challenged acts occurred in a private or public place did have meaning. But, again the significance to the dissent was one of looking at the entire context. So it was that Justice Bastarache both itemized relevant factors going to establish context and then addressed the question of public or private place where the acts took place. He wrote:

> It can be seen from this Court's case law on indecency and obscenity that the following contextual factors may be taken into consideration in determining the standard of tolerance: (1) the private or public nature of the place; (2) the type of participants and the composition of the audience; (3) the nature of the warning given regarding the acts; (4) the measures taken to limit access to the place; (5) the commercial nature of the place and the acts; (6) the purpose of the acts; (7) the conduct of the participants; and (8) harm suffered by the participants.... This list is not exhaustive, however.

First, Justice Bastarache referred to the expert testimony of Dr. Campbell. (Following examination by counsel before the trial court, Dr. Campbell was deemed qualified to offer testimony as to the acts and behaviour in question.) In effect, Justice Bastarache said, the expert testimony demonstrated that the level of community tolerance varies in part on whether the act challenged is public or private. Dr. Campbell's testimony and its impact was summarized by the municipal court (the trial court):

However, the Court understands from Dr. Campbell's testimony that for Canadians, in all cases, swinging is understood to mean that the swapping of sexual partners is done in private, that is, "among themselves." The witness referred to a kind of "social contract" that is entered into, tacitly or specifically, between those who wish to participate in swapping. Thus, the more closed and off-limits the "social contract" is to third parties, the closer it is to falling within the "classical" definition of swinging. According to the witness, this is where the threshold of the contemporary Canadian community lies, that is, on the condition that the sexual activities take place in private.

Similarly, if the sexual activities take place in public, what is happening is no longer "swinging," but an "orgy." According to Dr. Campbell, Canadians clearly do not tolerate orgies and do not accept that other Canadians, even informed and consenting adults, participate in them.

Dr. Campbell confirmed this approach several times in his testimony at trial.

It was not enough, Justice Bastarache said, for the accused to limit the ability of patrons to "circulate freely within the confines of the establishment." To view the matter in context requires more. He wrote:

For these reasons, a swingers' club cannot automatically be characterized as a "private" place on the basis that the general public is not permitted to circulate freely within it. The place may retain a public dimension that is sufficient to support a finding of indecency.

If the contrary position were adopted, it would be impossible, provided that the participants consent and that the spectators are considered only to be participants, to sanction any sexual act that is not degrading or harmful to the participants. As we have seen, this unacceptable solution amounts to denying that the standard of tolerance can be applied to sexual acts performed in establishments that are accessible to the public. Such a solution does not take into account the fact that indecency is based on what Canadians do not abide other Canadians seeing or doing.... It would also amount to saying that only the morality of the participants themselves is relevant.

THE DISSENT: APPLYING A STANDARD OF COMMUNITY TOLERANCE TO THE FACTS

The dissent zeroed in on the application of the tolerance test to the facts. It found no room for doubt that either so-called privacy or consent of those participating shielded the accused from a finding of indecency under section 210(1) of the Criminal Code. We quote that portion of the dissent in some detail:

An analysis of the place where the acts were performed shows that the establishment is a public one. Although advertised as a private club, l'Orage was a place to which the public had ready access by invitation, express or implied.... Several facts illustrate this public dimension and the ease with which the public could enter the establishment. It should be noted that, despite the measures allegedly taken to limit access, members of the general public were on many occasions invited to join the club and to take part in sexual activities on the third floor.

The number of people who had access to the establishment and, potentially, to the third floor was also very high, about 800. All that was necessary to gain access to the establishment was to pay the requested fee after a cursory interview that was quite superficial. It was even easier to gain access to the establishment and to the third floor simply as the guest of a club member. Neither the [accused] nor his employees interviewed guests or gave them an official warning. They merely relied on the members to tell their guests about the exact nature of the sexual acts taking place on the third floor and to ensure that those guests shared the philosophy of partner swapping and would not be shocked by what they saw....

The majority's reasons for judgment appear to indicate that since the "public" in [this] case consisted solely of club members and their guests, the "general public" was at no risk of seeing the acts in question. We cannot subscribe to this interpretation. The "public" in [this] case consisted of people who were both participants and spectators. A place can be sufficiently public even though the people gathered there are members of a "private" club or the guests of members.... *The fundamental issue remains whether the community tolerates having these individuals witness these activities or take part in them in this context* [emphasis added].

In [this] case, the [accused] claims to have set up an adequate system for limiting access to the establishment and to the third floor to individuals who shared the philosophy of partner swapping and who knew what to expect when they entered the establishment. Our colleagues agree with him that the initial interview, the membership fees, the doorman on the first floor, the word "Privé" (private) on the door leading to the third floor and the [combination] lock on the door to the [accused's] apartment were effective and appropriate measures for controlling access.

With respect, these conclusions contradict the trial judge's findings, and we see no fatal error in her analysis. The interview with prospective members served merely to answer their questions, they were given no warning or official explanation regarding the sexual acts taking place in the establishment, and the veracity of their statements was not verified. The membership fees only confirm the commercial nature of the place and of the impugned acts, as we will see below. The purpose for which the money was collected is irrelevant, as the only material question is whether it was necessary to pay to take part in the acts. The notice on the door to the third floor was just as ineffective, since there was, as the trial judge indicated, a constant flow of people between the establishment's three floors. The trial judge pointed out that the third floor was a dependency of the two lower floors.... Finally, the evidence shows that all club members were given the combination to the lock on the apartment door upon joining the club and that they were all free to take guests there. In short, these measures did not adequately limit the public's access to a place where very explicit sexual acts were performed. In our view, the degree of privacy was therefore insufficient.

An analysis of the establishment's operations reveals the commercial nature of the activities that took place there. Several of the facts mentioned above testify to the commercial nature of the [accused's] business. Sexual acts could be performed on the third level of the establishment only after a mandatory commercial transaction between the participants and the owner of the establishment, since everyone had to pay a fee to become a member. The participants essentially purchased sexual services provided by other participants....

Canadians are not inclined to tolerate the commercial exploitation of sexual activities, which is contrary to a number of values of the Canadian community, such as equality, liberty and human dignity. The existence of facts that appear to be indicative of the commercial exploitation of sexual acts, while not in itself sufficient to support a finding of indecency, does clearly support the conclusion that the community standard of tolerance has been offended in [this] case. Under s. 210(1), whether or not social harm has been sustained is not a determinative factor in establishing indecency. It may, however, assist in gauging the degree of community tolerance when humiliating, degrading or demeaning acts are performed.

In [this] case, it is still possible to conclude that a form of social harm has been sustained that indicates that the level of tolerance of Canadians has been exceeded. This harm results from the failure to meet the minimum standards of public morality rather than from incompatibility with the "proper functioning of society" or from predisposing others to anti-social behaviour. This conclusion is

specific to s. 210(1) and results from the establishment of the standard of tolerance on the basis of an
objective, contextual analysis of the sexual acts.

Thus, an analysis of the context in which the
acts took place may make up for the absence of
harm as defined by the majority, as whether or not
such harm has been sustained is just one of the factors to be considered. In [this] case, the public and
commercial dimensions of the sexual practices in
issue would lead to the conclusion that those practices were indecent even if there were no harm.

In [this] case, the sexual acts were very explicit
acts, and they took place in a commercial establishment that was easily accessible to the general public. This situation caused a certain form of social
harm resulting from the failure to meet the minimum standards of public morality. In light of these
contextual factors, we are of the opinion that the sexual acts performed in the [accused's] establishment
clearly offended the Canadian community standard
of tolerance and were therefore indecent. Our analysis does not permit us to conclude that the Canadian
community would tolerate the performance, in a
commercial establishment to which the public has
easy access, of group sexual activities on the scale
of those that took place in this case. The [accused's]
establishment is therefore a common bawdy-house
within the meaning of s. 210(1).

YOU BE THE JUDGE

ANOTHER GROUND FOR INDECENCY?

The issue in this case was raised in *The Queen v. Labaye.*

THE FACTS

The Jester is a bar and fast food outlet located in an area of downtown Vancouver frequented by prostitutes and used for the sale and injection of drugs. The rate of HIV infection is several times greater in this area than in the rest of the city, the province or, for that matter, the rest of the nation.

Fred and Daisy, the new owners of The Jester, are anxious to increase profits. They have been careful to prevent the sale or use of drugs in the bar, and they have stopped solicitation by sex trade workers. Also, through careful surveillance, they have limited patronage to adults only.

Fred and Daisy want to provide a "forum" for what they call "openness" in their adult-only establishment. Consenting patrons will be able to dress (or undress) and behave as they want — as long as they do not injure themselves or others. A private area, physically separate from the street level entrance, will be made available for members only. It will be a place where explicit sex could take place — again only between consenting adults.

Such individuals will have to pay annual dues of fifty dollars and be interviewed to ensure that they understand the nature of the private area. In any event, the area will be accessible only (1) by interview to guarantee that is indeed where individuals want to go, and (2) by two locks, the combinations of which only members will know. No guests will be permitted. Membership will be limited to five hundred. No recording equipment of any kind will be allowed.

To the police and health authorities, however, the "private area" of The Jester, if allowed to function, poses a real problem. To them, there is a risk of sexual transmitted disease and especially HIV infection.

Fred and Daisy decide to proceed with the planned club, including the so-called "private area." It is that area which becomes the centre of the Crown's charge against them under the Criminal Code.

THE ISSUE

May the "private area" of The Jester be prohibited on the basis that it would be "indecent" due to the real risk to public health of sexually transmitted disease?

POINTS TO CONSIDER

- Under section 210(1) of the Criminal Code, it is an offence, punishable by two years in prison, to keep a common bawdy-house.
- A bawdy-house is defined in section 197(1) of the Code as a place kept, occupied, or resorted to by "one or more persons for the purpose of prostitution or the practice of acts of indecency."
- The Crown does not argue that prostitution took place in the "private area." No money was paid or received by those taking part in the sexual acts.
- The Jester, itself, is a "public place," although the

so-called "private area" is open only to screened members.

- Explicit sex did indeed take place in the "private area." The acts involved were numerous.
- Expert evidence from physicians and public health officials left no doubt there was danger that sexually transmitted disease would be passed on as a result of such explicit sex. In that sense, there was harm to those participating as well as the public.

DISCUSSION

The issue of sexually transmitted disease was raised in the Labaye case as a separate ground for finding explicit sex indecent. The Supreme Court, in its 7–2 decision, rejected the argument. It did not dispute the health dangers that might arise from such activity. Rather, Chief Justice McLachlin, speaking for the Court, in effect said that the danger was *not relevant to the question as to whether the acts in question were indecent.*

The chief justice wrote:

> A form of harm to participants that invokes special considerations is the danger of sexually transmitted disease. Clearly this is an important harm that may flow from sexual conduct. It has been considered as a factor in determining whether conduct is criminally indecent, and as a factor exacerbating an already existing harm....
>
> However, it is difficult to assign the risk

of sexually transmitted disease an independent role in the test for indecency. The risk of disease, while it may be connected to other legal consequences, is not logically related to the question of whether conduct is indecent, either conceptually or causally. *Indecency connotes sexual mores rather than health concerns, and sex that is not indecent can transmit disease while indecent sex might not* [emphasis added].

Let's pause for a moment to understand what the chief justice said and didn't say. First, she made it clear that *the danger of sexually transmitted disease, by itself, will not support a finding that an act is indecent.* However, the danger of sexually transmitted disease may be an element in the context of proving an act is indecent. And, it may add to the proof of existing harm. Finally, the chief justice did not rule out the possibility that the danger of sexually transmitted disease might not give rise to other violations of law, even the criminal law.

THE DISSENT

As noted, Justices Bastarache and LeBel dissented from the Court's opinion in the Labaye case. On the question of sexually transmitted disease, Justice Bastarache, who wrote the dissent, stated:

Harm to the participants is also relevant. Attention must therefore be paid to the risk of physical or psychological harm. This approach permits the risk of spreading sexually transmitted diseases ("STDs") to be taken into account. If the evidence demonstrates a real risk of transmission linked to the systematic absence of protective measures, this factor will be relevant. We do not agree with the majority on this point, since Canadians' tolerance of sexual practices is influenced by the risks of spreading STDs.

In support of his view, Justice Bastarache cited *The Queen v. Tremblay,* [1993] 2 *Supreme Court of Canada Reports* 932. There the Court refused to find an act of a nude female dancer indecent in part because she had *no physical contact with customers.* The Court stated:

Although the lack of physical contact is not determinative of the issue [of finding indecency within the meaning of the Criminal Code], it is nonetheless highly significant. The rule [of the establishment where she danced] ensured that there would be little likelihood that physical harm or hurt would be done to either individual. Of equal importance was that it ensured that the transmission of infectious sexual diseases was prevented. This factor should increase the level of the tolerance of the community for the acts performed at The Pussy Cat.

CHALLENGE QUESTION

DEBATE AFTER THE SUPREME COURT'S DECISION?

Q: Following the Supreme Court of Canada's decision in The Queen v. Labaye, what role, if any, does Parliament have in modifying that portion of the Criminal Code relating to "indecency"?

Bear in mind that the decisions of the Supreme Court of Canada reflect the supreme law of the land. And, it should be noted that the Charter of Rights and Freedoms is part of the Constitution of Canada and, as such, embodies guarantees and values which, in certain instances, courts and government must honour and, in other situations, judges may be called upon in interpreting the meaning of laws, such as the Criminal Code.

In the Labaye case, the Supreme Court was called upon to interpret the meaning of "indecency." The provision of the Criminal Code in which it appeared did not specifically define the term. The Court found meaning by looking to past cases and those fundamental values reflected in the Charter.

The decision, as such, leaves it open to Parliament and the citizenry to engage in a discussion as to whether the statutory meaning of "indecency" should be changed, for example, to reflect "community standards of tolerance." This is not to say that any change in that regard would not in turn raise questions under the Charter. But, it is to say that the door is open for Parliamentary action. That action could include enactment of a law which specifically incorporates the community standard of tolerance. Again, recall that, as a matter of interpretation, the Court majority in the Labaye case rejected that standard in favour of a *harm-based test*.

THE DECISION: A START FOR DISCUSSION?

In an editorial, the *Globe and Mail* argued for just such a debate. It stated:

> It shouldn't be impossible for a liberal society to tolerate diversity without abandoning common values and standards. It shouldn't be impossible to say that, while people do get divorced, stable marriages and families that stay together are a foundation stone of a healthy society. It shouldn't be impossible to say that while people can do what they like in their own homes, it offends and degrades the community when group-sex parties are allowed in neighbourhood bars....
>
> The Supreme Court's groundbreaking decision is a good starting point for a real debate. What does community mean in the modern world? What is the role of the state, if any, in regulating morality? Is there even such a thing as public morals in a modern society? (*Globe and Mail*, January 3, 2006)

THE PRESS RESPONDS: DIFFERENT VIEWS

The Supreme Court of Canada's decision in *The Queen v. Labaye* resulted in substantial comment in the press. We have included two excerpts and cited others.

GLOBE AND MAIL

Cold country, hot sex. The *Economist* will love us. The Europeans will sing our praises. The Americans will denounce us even as they book their hotel reservations. But as a matter of law, the Supreme Court of Canada's 7–2 ruling [in the Labaye case], legalizing most sex clubs and throwing out the community test of tolerance, makes no sense.

Oh, it was an ultra-modern, superbly tolerant philosophical treatise — under such high-flown headings as "Toward a Theory of Harm" — but it collapses under scrutiny. For one thing, it sets an impossible standard for dealing with sex clubs: proof of harm verging on social disorder. For another, it describes as private places clubs that are licensed bars in commercial buildings, that advertise in newspapers and magazines, and that send out thousands of brochures. For a third, it undermines the very notion that the criminal law should be regulating morality....

This is about much more than sex. It is about the uses to which the criminal law may be put. Should the Criminal Code be used to legislate morality or ethics or, oh archaic word, decency? ... The commercializing of sex in public places may offend community standards, and the courts should not be afraid to say so (*Globe and Mail*, December 22, 2005).

LE QUÉBÉCOIS LIBRE

While it seems painfully obvious that swinging must increase the stresses on a relationship, it is also obvious that some people are much better than others at handling stress. Even more telling, some people are good at handling one kind of stress and therefore make good police officers, for example, but would flounder trying to handle the kinds of stresses a grade three teacher navigates with grace. People are different, and it is certainly plausible that for some couples who are better able to deal with the particular stresses of swinging, the benefits might just outweigh the costs.

You don't need to be a libertarian to applaud the Supreme Court in this instance. You just need to be willing to tolerate the choices other people make even when you disagree with those choices. You need to be willing to let people fall down once in a while rather than treat them like little children unable to assume any measure of personal responsibility. And, you need to be willing at least to entertain the possibility that maybe, just maybe, you don't know with one hundred percent certainty what's best for everyone else — a little tolerance, a helping of individual responsibility, and a touch of humility (*Le Québécois Libre,* January 15, 2006).

(*Globe and Mail,* December 27, 2005; *Winnipeg Free Press,* January 8, 2006)

REFERENCES AND FURTHER READING

Blackwell, Richard. "Top Court Redefines Obscenity." *Globe and Mail,* December 22, 2005.

Buckingham, Janet Epp. "The Supreme Court Swingers Decision Strips Away Community Values." *Globe and Mail,* December 27, 2005.

Doucet, Bradley. "Supreme Court Strikes a Blow for Swingers' Rights." *Le Québécois Libre,* January 15, 2006.

Globe and Mail. "Just Like That, There Go Community Standards.", December 22, 2005.

_____. "Of Norms and Morals." , January 3, 2006.

Jantz, Harold. "Moral Confusion — No Harm from Swingers' Clubs? Really?" *Winnipeg Free Press,* January 8, 2006.

Moore, Oliver. "Swingers' Clubs Hope Ruling Will Help Stimulate Their Business." *Globe and Mail,* December 23, 2005.

Peritz, Ingrid. "Swinger Hot Spot Declares Victory." *Globe and Mail,* December 22, 2005.

INDEX

COMING JANUARY 2015 IN THE
UNDERSTANDING CANADIAN LAW SERIES:

Crime Scene Investigations
By Daniel J. Baum

When police are called in to investigate a crime, what powers
and limitations apply to them? What are their rights to question
strangers, search without warrants, or detain individuals who
might become suspects? *Crime Scene Investigations* breaks down
the Supreme Court's decisions on questions like these into clear
and practical terms.

The line between a lawful search and an improper one can
be dangerously thin, and officers can be held accountable for any
wrongdoing, intentional or not. The controversy surrounding such
techniques as "stop-and-frisk" sweeps and compulsory DNA test-
ing underscores the importance of understanding the legal dimensions of police powers. Because interactions between law enforcement officers and civilians are often charged with complexities,
Crime Scene Investigations provides a level-headed guide, indis-
pensable for those on either side of an investigation.

ALSO IN THE UNDERSTANDING CANADIAN LAW SERIES:

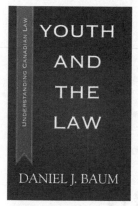

Youth and the Law
By Daniel J. Baum

Laws, as they relate to youth and youth issues, can be difficult to understand for those they are intended to serve. In the first book of the Understanding Canadian Law series, author Daniel J. Baum breaks down the Supreme Court of Canada's decisions relating to youth in plain language intended for readers of all ages.

Drawing on examples from recent Supreme Court rulings, *Youth and the Law* walks the reader through such controversial subjects as spanking, bullying, youth violence, and police in the schools. Each chapter contains prompts to encourage critical thinking.

Youth and the Law is an objective introduction for all readers to better understand how law impacts the young.

Available at your favourite bookseller

DUNDURN

VISIT US AT
Dundurn.com
@dundurnpress
Facebook.com/dundurnpress
Pinterest.com/dundurnpress